Trees bow to form
a leafy tunnel outside
Pont-l'Évêque,
Normandy.

getaway

The wind kicks up at Los Cerritos Beach in Baja California Sur, Mexico.

getaway

food & drink to transport you

renee erickson
with sara dickerman

photography by jim henkens
illustrations by jeffry mitchell

ABRAMS, NEW YORK

For Dan, my favorite person
to explore the world with, but with whom
I am happiest cooking in our backyard

Dessert at Rochelle Canteen,
London

Foxgloves at London's Columbia Road Flower Market

foreword

When I stumbled across Renee's first book, *A Boat, a Whale & a Walrus: Menus and Stories*, in a London bookshop, I could feel my body fill with warmth and little somersaults of excitement, the same feeling I experience when sitting down to a table of food with friends. I showed her book to other cooks and food lovers—and also to my own publishers as a way of conveying, without using words, the sensibility that I wanted my own books to have. I felt that Renee was a kindred spirit, a twin that I had somehow lost and now had found.

Social media makes meeting your heroes possible, and so I got to know Renee (the first time we exchanged messages I had to pinch myself—Renee Erickson was writing to *me?*) and then spent time with her in both London and Seattle. Before I visited her Seattle restaurant, the Walrus and the Carpenter, it was on my list of "top ten places to eat in the whole world." When I got there, I loved it, not just for the food but also for Renee's style.

I've been waiting for another book from her for what seems like ages, and *Getaway* seems perfect for our times. As she finished writing it, we were all dealing with a world that had become smaller. COVID-19 had forced confinement. We had to stay in our own countries, cities, towns, even in our own homes.

I did very little traveling as I was growing up but for different reasons. My early childhood was spent in 1970s Northern Ireland; it was expensive to travel outside Ireland, especially if, like us, you were a family of six, so we stayed within our own shores. I read about places and cooked food from other countries as a way of getting around the world. I wish I'd had *Getaway* all those years ago because it gives you three things: a strong sense of place, inviting you to travel with your mind; recipes—vibrant and doable—that will bring these places into your own kitchen; a guide that will help you plan your own journeys—even if they're in the distant future. I'm only sorry the book isn't longer.

Renee doesn't travel to tick off countries or Michelin-starred restaurants. Her traveling is slower, and it isn't just about food. She notices small details: the light in a particular restaurant, the glassware, the pattern on the floor. She soaks up all the simple things that make life rich, and she tells you about them. She also amasses knowledge. In *Getaway* you can drink in the London gin scene, learn how to make a really good French tartine, and think again about colombage, the half-timbered construction of so many buildings in Normandy.

Right now, as the rain on a dreary London day hammers the windows of my kitchen, *Getaway* is helping me to travel. I've made Renee's Currant and Hazelnut Anchoïade with Crudités (page 97) and, as I eat and read, I'm walking round Paris with her. When we are able to actually go places again, this book will be in my suitcase and Renee's voice will be in my head.

—*Diana Henry (August 2020)*

Chef Taylor Thornhill of Bateau foraging in the forest
with his sons, Bernat and Lucian

preface

The photographs and recipes for this book were created before the COVID-19 crisis hit, and before the deaths of Ahmaud Arbery, George Floyd, and Breonna Taylor sparked a momentous, nationwide reckoning with race. As I flip through its pages now, I can't imagine what our lives will look like in the next few years. Not only does travel feel like a distant memory, but our society, including restaurants and bars themselves, has been completely devastated by the year's events, and we are grappling with the future of our country.

The uncertainty about the future of travel, the economy, and restaurant culture in general makes me cherish the memories of those trips even more. I hope I have captured, in some part, the specialness of these places, and that we may all have the opportunity to visit them again sometime very soon.

I feel so tied to the people and the places in this book, especially in times of disruption like this; my fellow chefs, servers, bartenders, purveyors, farmers, fishermen, cheesemakers, and winemakers around the world are part of my larger family.

As I write, I have had to close several of our restaurants, uncertain when we will be able to get back to work, and, once we do, if we can stay open. What has not changed, however, is my deep connection to the comfort and joy that comes from feeding people.

Looking forward, we as a company at Sea Creatures, my restaurant group, have committed to unflinching evaluation of our organization and meaningful change-making to be more employee-centric, anti-racist, and resilient in the face of today's challenges. We have partnered with organizations like Restaurants for Change and One Fair Wage to share knowledge and advocate for positive change for restaurant employees across the country. Our world is hurting and we want to be part of the wave that makes it better for all. And every so often, I can share a bit of food with my husband, Dan (who also runs a restaurant), at the home where we spend so little time right now.

This book feels all the sweeter, both as a collection of good memories and as a guidebook for you, my readers, to learn to make the food I love at home. At first it might be for just your household, but as our circles widen once again, I hope that it makes for many sweet memories to come.

—*Renee (September 2020)*

introduction

Travel with me, and I'm likely to make you walk through the farmers' market, not once but twice—okay, maybe three times. We may get a little lost, because at some point, I'll put my phone in my pocket and start following my gut. We may also sit down a good bit. I can spend hours observing the scene from a sidewalk café or a park bench. Some food-oriented travelers are like trophy hunters, investing their energies in pouncing on the latest, hottest restaurants. That's not exactly my style. My own approach is slower paced, driven by curiosity and a purposeful patience. I don't want to lose myself in the rush to see everything in one visit; I take my time and try to observe the details—in art, style, food, and personal interactions—that come together to create a culture.

My first book, *A Boat, a Whale & a Walrus*, celebrated the people—mostly based here in the Pacific Northwest—who helped shape my cooking life. This book extends itself a little farther afield. I'll introduce you to my favorite places and the friends I've made along the way. I'll reveal locales to eat and shop, celebrate go-to ingredients from each destination, and in pictures and stories, try to capture some of the spirit of each place.

But just as important, I want to show you what I bring back from these trips, because, after all, travel is my favorite teacher. So there are detailed guides to my favorite ingredients and techniques that I have been taught, and, of course, recipes—for approachable cocktails and food—that can be made anywhere you happen to live but that help embody the spirit of these special places.

Ever since I lived in Rome as an undergraduate art student, travel has been a key part of my imagination and my identity. Somehow, I became the chef of a family of restaurants in Seattle, Washington, that includes the Walrus and the Carpenter, Bateau, the Whale Wins, Willmott's Ghost, Deep Dive, Bistro Shirlee, Barnacle, Westward, General Porpoise Doughnuts, Bar Melusine, and Great State Burger. To keep those places feeling fresh and inviting, I am always seeking inspiration for menus, for design, and for something less concrete: how to make sure they stay warm, relaxing spaces.

This part of my life and my career only gets more important as time goes by. Creating restaurants is really about designing welcoming settings for people to connect. Travel allows me to

Il Goccetto, a favorite wine bar in Rome

see what puts people at ease and what delights them all at once. Details—like a comfortable banquette where an extra friend can slide into a table or the beautiful way my Baja-based friend Dano trims a lime into a square, then perches the whole thing as the garnish on the lip of a margarita glass—fuel my understanding of those spaces where I find the most comfort, so that I can use these lessons in other, often very different environments.

I've found, whether I'm in England or Italy or France or Mexico, that I'm drawn to places where people look most at ease: those informal, bustling spaces like cafés and street-side bars where even a tourist like me feels like I'm a part of the living city. I like to watch people greet each other, to listen to the flow of conversations, and to nibble on a salty snack while lingering over sparkling spritzes. It delights me to see people gathering in the real world.

Timing is important, too: Often those places are most compelling during what the French call *l'heure de l'apéritif,* but this in-between time, neither lunch nor dinner, has parallels in many other countries. In Roman street cafés at the *aperitivo* hour, or in bayside taco stands in Baja California, there's a casual ease to getting a bite in the late afternoon or early evening.

At home I love to start entertaining in that late-afternoon time, too—it's a relaxed moment in the day, and of course, late-afternoon light is so beautiful. And I've found the best things to cook at home are often the least complicated. Fancy dinners are delightful, but serving simple, inviting appetizers makes a gathering feel more relaxed for guests and hosts alike.

In making this book, I was grateful to have the opportunity to revisit my favorite destinations, and then to create recipes for you in my own Pacific Northwest kitchen to conjure a sense of each place. You'll find chapters on the places I've returned to most in my life: Rome, Paris, Normandy, London, Baja California, and Seattle, with stories and recipes for sharing drinks and delicious food.

This cookbook is meant to encourage you to create your own easy, welcoming spaces at home, no matter where you live. I hope you'll find a new easy mode for feeding your friends and family. When I have people over, things tend to be sketched out—not too precisely planned. Half the time, I'm still dusting dirt off my knees from gardening when people show up. I might welcome friends with something like fresh dill dip and chips, or a hunk of grilled bread smoothed over with whipped ricotta and herbs. I'll very likely make a simple vermouth cocktail or a spritz and toss a blossom from the garden into each glass. We might stop there and just hang out over snacks, or I might put everyone to work to make a few heartier plates to share.

Having people over has, of course, changed in the past year, and this food is just right for adapting with the times. Even before the pandemic, I loved entertaining outside, but now doorstep drinks and picnics seem even smarter. Sharing might even mean preparing homemade crackers and delivering them to a neighbor's door with some ripe Stilton and a cocktail kit. To be flexible, I've provided recipes in this book that work for an impromptu drinks-and-snacks *aperitivo* hour, and also some heartier, but still relaxed recipes, if you want to stretch out your time together.

I hope this book gets you dreaming about travel, but you don't need to go anywhere to feel transported. *Getaway* is an invitation to create relaxed moments with housemates, family, or friends, centered on delicious but not-too-intricate cocktails and food. Enjoy it in good company!

That's me in Normandy with a big old salad and a garden full of roses.

how to use this book

what i mean when i say "salt" and other tips

Here is some general information about this book, as well as my guide to some ingredients and techniques that thread their way throughout the recipes.

SERVINGS
Since this book is about serving friends without making formal entrées for individual diners, the number of servings is a bit tricky to calculate. Unless marked otherwise, assume I am thinking about hearty appetizers when I suggest how many servings each recipe makes.

OLIVE OIL
I cook with a lot of olive oil—it's a cooking medium and a seasoning, and I love to keep a lot of options on hand in my pantry. Here's the basic breakdown, though. If I call for "olive oil," I mean extra-virgin olive oil, but not the super-precious stuff—find a brand of good Spanish, Moroccan, or Italian olive oil that doesn't cost an arm and a leg (Atlas Organic brand from Morocco is what we love and use in all Sea Creatures restaurants). Then, you also want to have a little bottle of really special stuff—in the book I'll call it "really good olive oil." That's the stuff that should be date-stamped from the past year and should be stored in the dark, far from the stove. Use it to dress salads or anoint burrata or a perfect summer tomato. I like too many to mention, but I especially love a good spicy Tuscan oil such as Selvapiana or Frescobaldi Laudemio.

SALT
I am not especially fussy about salt. No table salt, of course—I'm not that unfussy. But I switch between kosher salt, which is always lurking around every kitchen I'm in, and sea salt, which I buy in its coarse, moist form (I like sea salt from Brittany) and grind in small batches with a mortar and pestle to be about the coarseness of kosher salt. There are a few times when I do almost always use kosher salt (pre-salting eggplants, for example), and in that case, I'll say kosher salt. Otherwise, I'll say salt, and let you use the amount and type of salt you like the best. I do like to keep some crunchy sea salt around as well, for adding texture as I finish a dish. In my recipes, I'll call that "crunchy sea salt." That might be

Maldon sea salt, with its delicate pyramid-shaped crystals, or lovely moist Fleur de Sel de Guérande. Use what you love.

GRILLING BREAD

I like a grill pan for making toast. The only trick is to make sure to do it right before serving—wait too long and your toast gets stale. Use a paper towel to rub a light coating of olive oil in the grooves of the pan and heat it over high heat. Cut bread into sturdy slices and brush it with a light coat of olive oil on each side. Lay the slices in a single layer and toast until they crisp nicely with dramatic grill marks, on the order of 2 or 3 minutes. Flip and grill the other side of each slice. Of course, if you have a hot grill going, you can grill your bread, too: You'll want to put it on a hot but not flaming part of the fire and watch very carefully.

TOASTING NUTS AND SEEDS

Toasting brings out the delicious warmth in nuts and can also reduce the tannic bite of walnuts and hazelnuts. There are two basic procedures for toasting: on the stovetop and in the oven. In either case, patience pays off—don't try to rush or you will end up with a pile of scorched nuts.

The stovetop is a good way to handle smaller nuts (like pistachios or pine nuts) and seeds. In a dry skillet over medium heat, pour in a single variety of seeds/nuts. Have a cool plate ready next to the stove. Swirl the seeds with a spoon or a shake of the wrist a few times every minute. Nuts are ready when they are slightly darkened and aromatic. Pumpkin seeds will pop to let you know they're ready.

To toast nuts in the oven, heat it to 300°F (150°C). Spread a single variety of nut on a baking sheet and let it toast, stirring them every 5 minutes or so. Nuts are ready when they are warmed through and slightly darker at their centers. Walnuts can take 12 to 15 minutes (depending on size and freshness), while smaller nuts will be done sooner. Don't store toasted nuts more than a day or two—they will lose their spark; before then keep them in an airtight container at room temperature.

MAKING CROSTINI

One long baguette should make about 25 to 30 crostini. To make them, heat the oven to 350°F (180°C). Cut the bread along the bias into ¼-inch (6-mm) slices. Place them in a single layer on one or two baking sheets and brush both sides of each slice with olive oil. Sprinkle with salt. Bake, turning the slices once during cooking, until the slices are crisp and light golden brown, about 12 to 15 minutes. Once cooled, crostini can keep for two days at room temperature in an airtight container.

HARD-BOILED EGGS
When I want an egg to have a little more structure, like when I am going to grate or devil it, I cook it this way: Place eggs in a medium pot, covered with 2 to 3 inches (5 to 7.5 cm) of water. Bring the water to a boil over medium-high heat. Turn off the heat, cover the pot, and set a timer for 12 minutes. Grab a medium bowl of ice water while the eggs are bathing in the hot water. When the timer goes off, scoop the eggs into the cold water to stop the cooking.

CHILLING COCKTAIL GLASSES
Warm glasses ruin cold cocktails. To chill them, you can place cocktail glasses in the freezer for at least 15 minutes, or if you are in a rush, fill them with ice and let them sit while you gather ingredients and prepare your cocktail.

SIMPLE SYRUP
Simple syrup is the most neutral way to add a bit of sweetness to a cocktail. To make it, use 1 cup (200 g) granulated sugar to 1 cup (240 ml) water. Heat them together in a small saucepan and stir until dissolved. Cool and keep in an airtight jar in the refrigerator for up to a week.

rome

amari, salumi, and salty bites

In truth, I first went to Rome for the art, not the food. I was a student at the University of Washington and signed up for its studio art program at the Palazzo Pio in the historic center of Rome. It was my first visit to Europe, and I planned to spend the semester gazing at the Roman columns, and the Berninis, and the Caravaggios, and making my own art back at the Palazzo. From the start, I was totally smitten with Rome; I still am. You can wander around and get a little lost in the narrow streets, and then you turn the corner and there's something glorious, like, say, the Pantheon. Rome is a labyrinth of beauty that always surprises me.

I have never lost my sense of wonder at the light in Rome: the look of late-afternoon sunlight on the ochre stucco walls, the shadows

cutting sharply across the narrow streets, the soft reflection of neon sheening on the dark cobblestones at night.

Rome also shifted my whole outlook on food. I was an art student with little money, and even when I couldn't afford to dine out much, daily walks through the market, sometimes just observing, tuned me into the seasons of food as never before. I'd never seen food so well tended and artfully displayed, and I can still picture that bright palette of vegetables: green beans, yellow squash blossoms, red tomatoes, purple eggplants. I also learned that a little bit of something luxurious can make a big impression—a few slices of good fennel with a ripe tomato and a hunk of bread could make for a feast.

I could always afford to enjoy a slice of pizza *al taglio*, Rome's chewy pizza cut to order with a pair of scissors, and so I regularly pressed my way into classic bakeries like Forno Campo de' Fiori to grab a slice. I had to learn to stand my ground: If I was timid, tiny grandmothers would keep scooting past me to the counter and spend forever picking out just the right loaf or cherry ricotta tart. And so I stood tall, pushed up close to the counter, and in my wobbly Italian asked for my pizza—usually bianca (without sauce). To this day, you won't see me hesitate at a food counter—I'll step right in to get what I'm craving.

I love the pace of Rome, too. Of course, traffic can be insane. If you go a day without almost being hit by a motor scooter, then you haven't been in Rome. But there is also a feeling that Romans know how to pause a moment to relish good company. Sometimes, it's that guy on the motor scooter having a quick red-light chat with a friend on the street. Or it's two people outside a government building, locked in intense dialogue, stepping toward each other, rather than away like Americans do. And of course, come the golden hour, the cafés fill up with animated people conversing over wine or spritzes that glow coral in the late-afternoon sun.

I was able to spend another good chunk of time in Rome more recently. When my husband, Dan, and I were newlyweds, we took almost a month there together. In the evening, we would make a point of having a glass at one of the center's great wine bars, like L'Angolo Divino or Il Goccetto. It's those wine bars more than the restaurants that are my jumping-off point when I entertain at home with Rome on my mind—I love pasta *amatriciana* and *cacio e pepe*, but truthfully, I rarely cook pasta at home. Instead I gather food that tastes great with wine or spritzes. Simple, intense, and satisfying bites of good cheese, marinated vegetables, olives, and salumi are just what you need to make the conversation roll on into the evening.

miss willmott's

2 ounces (60 ml) Amara
    Amaro
2 ounces (60 ml) Amaro
    Nardini
1½ ounces (45 ml) Blood
    Orange Shrub (see Note)
4 ounces (120 ml) dry
    prosecco
2 blood orange slices,
    to garnish

Makes 2 cocktails

When I was asked to create a restaurant in the Spheres, the incredible glass-walled conservatory built at Amazon's head-quarters, I looked for a connection between the gardens and the Italian food I wanted to serve. I uncovered a Brit-ish Italophile, the horticulturist Ellen Willmott, and named the restaurant after a pretty thistle that bears her name: Willmott's Ghost. I'd have loved to know her. She traveled the world to discover new species of plants and supposedly would walk around other people's gardens with the seeds of favorite plants in her pockets—pockets with intentional holes in them! Like me, she surrounded herself with beau-tiful food and she had a love of wine and puppies. I admire her sense of playfulness and passionate interest in things that also matter so much to me. With a shot of blood-orange shrub (a sweetened drinking vinegar), this drink is spirited and tart, just like her.

Have ready two old-fashioned glasses, each with one large ice cube. Fill a cocktail shaker with ice and then add the Amara Amaro, Amaro Nardini, and the shrub. Cover and shake hard for 30 seconds. Strain into the prepared glasses. Top with the prosecco. Lay an orange slice on each ice cube.

Note: If you want to make your own shrub, combine 1 cup (240 ml) blood orange juice with 1 cup (200 g) sugar in a jar. Stir well and let sit until the sugar is dissolved, and then add 1 cup (240 ml) apple cider vinegar. Store in an airtight jar in the refrigerator for up to 2 weeks. Shrub and Co. makes a nice one if you want to purchase it instead.

the warley place

4 ounces (115 g) fresh basil
1 (750-ml) bottle L.N. Mattei
    Cap Corse Blanc
    Quinquina
Crushed ice (see Note)
2 ounces (60 ml) Spumante
    Rosé
Basil leaves, to garnish
Lemon wheel, to garnish

Makes 1 cocktail

This drink is named after the Essex garden and home of Ellen Willmott. During her lifetime, Ellen was said to have grown and catalogued nearly one hundred thousand species of plants. While the buildings on the once-lush estate have been pulled down, and the nature reserve now there bears little trace of the ponds, rock gardens, and flower beds she once maintained, this herbaceous and summery spritz is a lasting tribute to her gardening skills. Cap Corse Blanc Quinquina is a floral aperitif from Corsica made bitter with quinquina and even more fragrant with an infusion of fresh basil! The pale rose and green of the drink is also a kind of pastel salute to the Italian flag, echoing the colors of the restaurant that bears her name.

In a carafe, combine the basil with the quinquina. Swirl, cover the top of the carafe, and leave to infuse in the refrigerator overnight. Wash and dry the quinquina bottle well. The next day, strain the liquid and pour back into the bottle to store. It will make 25 ounces (750 ml) syrup and can be stored in the refrigerator for up to 1 week.

Fill a rocks glass with crushed ice and pour in 1½ ounces (45 ml) basil-infused quinquina. Top with the Spumante Rosé and garnish with the basil and lemon.

Note: You can crush ice for a drink or two in a clean kitchen towel. Simply wrap the cubes from an ice tray in the towel and bang with a wooden spoon or rolling pin. If you get in the habit, however, it's nice to have a sturdier canvas ice-crushing Lewis bag and a wooden mallet. They are easy to source online at places like cocktailkingdom.com.

apricot and bay leaf bellini

My friend Carrie Omegna, who runs our company (also taught me everything I know about wine), joined me in Venice several years ago. I insisted we go to Harry's Bar, the classic restaurant near the water, and also the birthplace of the Bellini. Even after all the attention over the years, Harry's is still really old-school Venice, filled with gleaming wood, white-jacketed waiters, and the well-dressed, suspiciously well-behaved children of fancy tourists. Everything was delicious, small, and very Italian, though we almost fainted when we saw the bill. Still, we were hooked—and I made Bellinis all summer long at my first restaurant, Boat Street Café, afterward—often with apricots instead of white peaches—any excuse to sneak in more stone fruit. Bellinis were always a pain because they would foam like crazy—until I discovered the trick of leaving the uncorked bottle of prosecco open in the fridge for fifteen minutes before mixing it with the fruit puree. Also, make sure everything is super cold before you start.

2 cups (310 g) washed, halved, and pitted apricots
1 bay leaf, lightly crushed
3 tablespoons sugar
1½ teaspoons lemon juice
1 (750-ml) bottle prosecco
1 to 2 apricots, cut into ½-inch (12-mm) wedges, to garnish

Makes 6 to 8 cocktails

First, make the apricot nectar: In a heavy-bottomed saucepan, combine the apricots, bay leaf, sugar, and ½ cup plus 2 tablespoons (150 ml) water. Bring to a boil over high heat. Reduce the heat and simmer until the apricots are totally soft and broken down, about 10 to 15 minutes.

Strain the apricot and liquid through a fine sieve, pushing the solids through with the back of a ladle. Discard the skins and bay leaf. Let cool completely, then store in an airtight container in the refrigerator (or in the freezer, thawing overnight in the fridge) until ready to use, up to 1 or 2 days.

Pour the nectar into a large, chilled pitcher. Slowly pour in the prosecco, letting it run down the side of the pitcher. Stir to combine, and pour into your glass of choice—flutes are pretty and traditional, but not essential. Garnish with a wedge of apricot on the rim of each glass. Keep any extra Bellinis in the fridge or over ice, but drink ASAP!

rossa sicily spritz

1½ ounces (45 ml) Amara
    Amaro
3 ounces (90 ml) prosecco
1½ ounces (45 ml) soda water
1 thick slice blood orange,
    halved
Paper straw (optional)

Makes 1 cocktail

Amara Amaro is a special bitter made in Sicily, where the citrus groves are legendary. Created with sustainably harvested blood oranges, it's bright, fragrant, and less cloying than many *aperitivi*. I had one of the more magical experiences of my life when I landed in Sicily for the first time. We drove forever through the Sicilian countryside to get to the Hotel Zash, whose main building is itself the color of blood orange juice. We checked in and were about to head out to the bar in the building next door, but the skies opened. We watched through the glass walls of our room as the rain pelted down and made the blooming orange grove tremble. After the rain subsided, we finally got to the bar. We had spritzes accompanied by deep-fried Calabrian chile gnocchi and olives. Everything had a rosy glow, from the spritzes to the sky to the volcano beyond.

Fill a wineglass halfway with ice. Pour in the Amara Amaro, then add the prosecco, soda, and the juice from one of the half-slices of orange. Stir very briefly and slip the other half-slice into the glass. Serve with a paper straw, if desired.

cocchi rosa americano

1½ ounces (45 ml) Carpano or
    Punt e Mes Vermouth
1½ ounces (45 ml) Cocchi
    Rosa
Soda water
Orange slice, to garnish
Lemon peel, to garnish

Makes 1 cocktail

When I have a drink in the afternoon—especially if I am traveling—I love to find something that's less boozy than an ever-tempting negroni. That way the drink won't make me *"un po* tipsy" and keep me from exploring more afterward. One delicious option is the negroni sbagliato, which replaces the gin in a negroni with prosecco. Another is an Americano, which swaps soda water for the gin. Effervescent drinks like this are just the crisp thing I crave with some afternoon charcuterie or olives. They are also a great, somewhat gentle, way to introduce a bitter to someone new to the world of aperitivi.

In a Collins glass half filled with ice, stir together the vermouth and the Cocchi Rosa. Top with soda water, stir, and garnish with an orange slice and a fresh twist of lemon peel.

Cocchi Rosa Americano

Two negronis and a spritz at the Roman wine bar Litro

the anatomy of a spritz

Spritz-o-mania has hit most of Europe and made inroads in the States as well. And no wonder—not too alcoholic, prettily pastel, and bubbly, spritzes invite conversation (and salty snacks!). I like spritzes, too, because they are easy to fine-tune to how bitter or alcoholic you want them to be.

You're most likely to see spritzes made with one of the twin giants of Italian bitters: Campari or Aperol. In truth I prefer some other bitters, especially wine-based bitters like Cappeletti, Contratto Americano Rosso, and Cocchi Americano Rosso. They are still bitter but are texturally softer than most spirit-based bitters. (There are always exceptions, of course, like the glorious blood orange Amara Amaro, made in Sicily.)

When it comes to prosecco, you want to get high-quality prosecco ideally from the Valdobbiadene DOCG, and make sure it is brut. Our house proseccos for spritzes are from Adami: the Garbèl or the slightly fancier Bosco di Gica. They are both tart and crisp with just the right amount of body to stand up to the bitters.

The method for making a spritz is simple. First, cool your glass down. No good cocktail was made in a dishwasher-warm glass. Swirl some ice in your glass to cool it quickly. Toss the cooling ice out! Extravagant, right? But this way the spritz won't get too watery with pre-melted ice.

Now add ice to the cool glass. Pour your amaro in first. It's dramatic to pour the amaro in last and watch the brightly colored liquid curl down through the ice cubes and into the prosecco, but if you have already filled the glass to near the top with prosecco, it's hard to adjust if you've made the drink too bitter or too sweet.

Add prosecco until you achieve the right color, which is something you will get a hang of as you make yourself more spritzes. The darker the color, the less prosecco, and the more bitter your drink will be. If you like an airier drink, add a splash of soda water and swirl. Now is the time for a pretty glass stirrer, if you've picked one up at a gift store somewhere, but even a chopstick will work.

Finish by adding a garnish—a slice of orange is nice, and so is a swath of orange zest twisted over the drink to express the oils, or a good wedge that you can squeeze into the spritz. Then, sip away.

It's always hard to choose among the delicious antipasti at Il Goccetto, a beloved wine bar in Rome.

antipasti naturalmente

The suitcase problem is real. Rome has some of the most exquisite specialty food stores in the world, including Roscioli Salumeria con Cucina. You walk in and the walls are shelved from floor to high ceiling with fancy foods: marinated artichokes, vinegars, dreamy capers, and, of course, exquisite olive oils. A refrigerator case holds the perishables—gorgonzola, *culatello*, and plump, bloomy-rind cheeses. But I panic slightly in a place like this, weighing the strong urge to purchase an exquisite jar of semidried tomatoes in olive oil or another of bitter orange marmalade, versus the need to actually be able to lift my suitcase into a taxicab. In the end, wine biscuits tend to win over too many heavy jars—not that I ever regret grabbing a special jar of marinated baby eggplant or tuna-stuffed olives.

Since it is a principle of mine to keep my pantry ready to go for impromptu celebrations, I can't do it with travel purchases alone. I shop for Italian imports here in Seattle: We have an extraordinary store called DeLaurenti where you can find the prettiest jars and potions (as well as killer prosciutto and cheeses). Online, sources like chefshop.com and zingermans.com also supply incredible preserved imports.

Here's what I try to keep in my cupboard: high-quality anchovies and sardines packed in olive oil, plus excellent butter beans, chickpeas, and borlottis. Also, jarred (never canned!) artichoke hearts, semi-dried tomatoes in oil, roasted eggplants, and stuffed olives and peppers. Good pistachios and walnuts are always welcome, and there are rarely enough crackers in the house: I like a mix of flaky saltine-style crackers and pretzel-ish *taralli*.

Some antipasti need to live in the refrigerator, of course. Thinly sliced prosciutto or culatello are a great start to any party, but you'll want them freshly sliced. For that reason, I like keeping a good, whole salami around, which doesn't risk drying out as quickly. Similarly, you can start a party over a fresh cheese like La Tur or mozzarella, but good aged Pecorino and, of course, Parmigiano-Reggiano keep for ages and are always ready to go. And finally, to dress things up, keep some delicious seasonings on hand—crunchy sea salt, acacia or chestnut honey, good Mediterranean chile flakes, wildly fragrant fennel pollen, and good capers in salt. And never forget olive oil, the greatest seasoning of all: I keep oil from a few regions on hand (see page 19 for more details).

When I set everything out, I typically reach for platters instead of boards for my antipasti: I like the contrast of the pretty plate with hearty food. And I don't offer too many choices: I'll typically have two kinds of cheese, something soft and something firm. I'll usually offer just one kind of meat, like that salami, though admittedly I'll throw in some mortadella, too, if I have it on hand, since I can never resist it. If the olive or veggie jars are pretty, I'll just use them to serve. I like lots of different vessels rather than one big platter with everything piled on it. Crackers and nuts will have their own dishes, and I'll put the oil, honey, pollen, or chile on the side in little bowls so people can try bites with and without the extra ingredient.

getting to the heart
of the artichoke

Give me an artichoke, in any form, and I'll appreciate it. I love them steamed, braised, roasted, pickled, and preserved. I even like them raw.

When I was studying in Rome, my friend Valerie and I were on a field trip to Florence when we got seriously hungry while walking somewhere near the Bardi Chapel. We saw a parade of construction workers in orange jumpsuits walk into a trattoria and followed them, sure they'd know where to find a good, moderately priced meal. As I looked at the menu, I saw *carciofi* there—I was thrilled! It is one my favorite vegetables (my mother loved to serve steamed artichokes—we would pull off the leaves and dip them in mayonnaise). But the menu said that the artichoke was served *crudo* (raw). I wasn't sure this was right—maybe it was an idiom. So I asked—"*Crudo?*" And the waiter said, "*Si, crudo.*" I asked a second time. And then a third. Each time he confirmed the artichoke would be raw. I was puzzled but assumed it was some kind of salad. I decided to be adventurous.

Five minutes later, the artichoke appeared: Whole. Raw. On a plate, with a lemon on it and a bowl of salt. I was stuck, no idea how to proceed, but thankfully one of the men in orange demonstrated for me.

It turns out that raw artichoke is crisp and a little astringent and a little nutty all at once—and it's excellent with steak. And

Parmigiano. Or, even better, steak and Parmigiano. And now I know the best way to prepare it.

If you are going to prepare an artichoke for eating raw (or for cooking), here's the way. Have a bowl full of water and squeeze a lemon into it. Keep the lemon on hand.

Pull back the outer leaves and snap them off one by one. Continue until there is a large pale section of more tender leaves exposed. Cut off about 1 inch (2.5 cm) from the top of the artichoke, eliminating any remaining tough bits. Rub with the half lemon and squeeze juice over the cut portions so they don't discolor.

Look into the center of the artichoke and find the fuzzy choke; if you can't see it, cut off a little more of the top of the artichoke. Using a paring knife and a small spoon, scoop out the choke and all the fuzzy bits, rubbing with lemon afterward.

Being very careful not to break the stem, use the paring knife (or a peeler) to shave off just the tough darker green layer of the stem. Trim the stem at the bottom about an inch (2.5 cm) from the bottom of the flower. Be careful to rub with more lemon juice on each freshly exposed surface of the artichoke. When you're finished, drop the artichoke into the lemon water and move on to the next.

roman-style artichokes with mozzarella

3 tablespoons chopped Italian parsley leaves
½ cup (15 g) torn fresh mint leaves plus 3 tablespoons chopped mint leaves
3 garlic cloves, minced
4 large artichokes, trimmed; soak in lemon water until ready to use (see page 39)
1 teaspoon salt
1 cup (240 ml) extra-virgin olive oil, plus more to garnish
2 balls fresh mozzarella di buffalo, about 8 ounces (225 g) each, thinly sliced
Crunchy sea salt, to finish
Ciabatta, for serving (optional)

Serves 4

If there is one vegetable people think of when they think of Rome, it's the artichoke. Fried *carciofi alla giudia* from Rome's Jewish quarter is extraordinary, but it's a bit tricky to master, so this braised version is a little more approachable, and it's a beloved staple throughout Rome.

In a small bowl, combine the parsley, chopped mint, and garlic. Pull the artichokes from the lemon water, sprinkle them with salt, and stuff them with the herb mixture.

In a heavy-bottomed pot, combine the olive oil, 1 cup (240 ml) water, and the artichokes, aiming their stems up, along with any leftover salt and herbs. Cover with a circle of parchment paper cut to fit the pot. Bring to a boil, then reduce the heat to a low simmer, cover the pot, and steam until tender, about 20 to 30 minutes.

Remove from the heat and let cool. The artichokes can be refrigerated for several days in the cooking liquid, but they should be served at room temperature.

To serve, arrange the mozzarella on a platter and sprinkle it with the crunchy sea salt. Arrange the artichokes on top, spooning some of the cooking juices around the plate. I love to have some crusty ciabatta bread to sop up all the olive oil.

oil-cured anchovy crostini with cultured butter

25 to 30 crostini (from one baguette, see page 20), at room temperature

1 cup (2 sticks/225 g) higher-fat unsalted butter, such as Kerrygold, cold

2 ounces (55 g) high-quality oil-cured anchovies (I like Ortiz)

Freshly ground black pepper, Controne hot pepper, and/or freshly grated lemon zest (optional)

Serves 6 to 8

It's rare that I would go out for a drink in Rome and not order anchovies: Rome is one place where anchovies are treated with the reverence they deserve, each fillet laid out smoothly in parallel to its neighbor. At Roscioli, there is even a section of the menu dedicated to different anchovy selections. And though Rome is awash in olive oil, most of the time, anchovies (even oil-marinated anchovies) are served, as here, with good butter. It is a gorgeous cushion for the saltiness of the anchovies. Don't skimp on the butter: I like to treat butter more like a good cheese than a flimsy spread.

Lay the crostini out on a serving tray. Slice the butter very thin and place a slice on each crostino. Place one deliciously oily anchovy fillet on each. The crostini are fabulous just so, but can also be tweaked by adding fresh black pepper, Controne hot pepper, and/or a little lemon zest as a garnish.

Seriously, almost every wine bar in Rome serves anchovy toast with butter: Here's the delicious stuff at Litro.

giardiniera

1 medium head of cauliflower, cut into small pieces

8 Fresno chiles, cored and seeded, sliced into thin rounds

1 fennel bulb, cored and sliced into ½-inch (12-mm) strips

3 carrots, peeled and cut into ¼ by 2-inch (6 mm by 5-cm) matchsticks

1 small yellow onion, chopped into medium dice

4 celery stalks, sliced across in ¼-inch (6-mm) pieces

½ cup (120 g) kosher salt

3 garlic cloves, thinly sliced

2 tablespoons dried Italian oregano

1 tablespoon chile flakes

5½ cups (1.3 L) extra-virgin olive oil

3½ cups (840 ml) white wine vinegar

2 teaspoons fennel seed

Makes 3½ quarts (3.3 L)

This mixed vegetable pickle is a very useful condiment. I love to snack on it with a salumi plate, and I also chop it up and whisk it into a red wine vinaigrette before dressing a salad—I like to think of it as bringing salad to the salad! Try the chunky dressing with a mix of bitter chicories and butter lettuce topped with a shower of shaved ricotta salata or Pecorino Romano. Homemade *giardiniera* is so crunchy and colorful. Make a big batch and have it on hand all year long, for times when fresh produce at the market is limited.

In a large bowl, combine the cauliflower, chiles, fennel, carrots, onion, and celery and toss with the salt. Cover and leave at room temperature overnight.

The next day, drain the saltwater from the vegetables and combine the vegetables with the garlic, oregano, chile flakes, olive oil, and vinegar. Cover and leave at room temperature overnight.

The next day, divide the fennel seeds among four 1-quart (1-L) jars. Using kitchen tongs, divide the vegetables evenly among the jars. Whisk the oil and vinegar remaining in the bowl and pour over the vegetables, dividing evenly. Cover the jars with their lids and refrigerate, letting the flavors combine for at least two days before using. Store for a month in the refrigerator. (This can be pressure canned, too, if you'd prefer to store outside the refrigerator and for a longer time.)

Ben Campbell, bread master, Wonder Dad

ben's focaccia al sale

I've tasted a million focaccia and was never a big fan until my head baker, Ben Campbell, developed his recipe for Willmott's Ghost. It's not flat and ropey like a lot of American focaccia, but fluffy, salty, and a happy sponge for lots of post-cooking olive oil. The flour does matter—you want stuff that is freshly milled with some germ in it, like Cairnspring Mills from Washington State. Look for good flour from your local mill, or the reliably fresh flours of King Arthur Flour. Though the focaccia at Willmott's is baked in special round pans, this one is adapted for the easy-to-find 9 by 13-inch (23 by 33-cm) pan.

2 cups (480 ml) warm water
2 teaspoons active dry yeast
5 cups (675 g) bread flour
2½ tablespoons sugar
2½ tablespoons milk powder
1 tablespoon kosher salt
12 tablespoons olive oil
    (175 ml), plus more for
    greasing and serving
1 tablespoon crunchy sea salt

*Makes one 9 by 13-inch
    (23 by 33-cm) focaccia*

In a stand mixer fitted with the dough hook, combine the warm water and yeast. In a large bowl, combine the flour, sugar, milk powder, and salt. After about 5 minutes, add the olive oil to the yeast mixture. With the machine running on low, gradually add the flour mixture. Continue mixing for about 2 minutes, until it comes together. Dump out onto a lightly floured surface and knead by hand for about 2 minutes.

Grease a large bowl with olive oil. Dump the dough into the bowl and cover with a towel. Place the dough in a warm, draft-free spot and let rise until doubled, about 2 hours.

Grease a 9 by 13-inch (23 by 33-cm) baking sheet with about ¼ cup (60 ml) of the olive oil. Dump the risen dough into the pan, turn it to make sure the top is well oiled, and use a combination of pressing and pulling to get the dough to the corners of the pan. Cover with plastic wrap and place in the refrigerator overnight. Two hours before serving, bring the dough out of the refrigerator to rise. Set a rack in the center of the oven and heat the oven to 500°F (260°C), using a pizza stone if you have it—you'll get much better spring in the focaccia.

When the dough has doubled in size, about an hour or so, push down with outspread fingers, making dimples in the dough. Drizzle with another ¼ cup (60 ml) of the olive oil and generously sprinkle with crunchy sea salt.

Bake until the crust is golden brown, about 15 to 20 minutes. If you can, wait until cooled to dig in. We serve this with plenty of extra oil poured on top, too.

ricotta and roasted cherry tomato crostini with too much olive oil

2 pounds (910 g) cherry
  tomatoes, on the vine
  if possible
3 tablespoons olive oil
Salt
1½ cups (340 g) whole-milk,
  basket-molded ricotta
¾ cup (180 ml) extra-virgin
  olive oil—the spicier, the
  better
1 teaspoon fennel pollen
6 thick slices great-quality
  handmade bread, grilled
  (see page 20)
Crunchy sea salt, to finish

Serves 6

This dish should be a delicious hodgepodge of indulgence, so simple but with every ingredient shining like a star. You need sweet cherry tomatoes, roasted until their flavors concentrate and almost start to candy, lush ricotta, and finally good, spicy olive oil to balance the richness and the acidity. Don't skimp on it.

Heat the oven to 425°F (220°C). In a bowl, toss the tomatoes with the olive oil and season with salt, then lay them on a baking sheet. Roast, shaking the pan every 10 minutes or so, until they start to break down and blacken in patches, about 30 minutes. Remove from the oven and let cool to room temperature.

Meanwhile, set out the ricotta about 20 minutes before you want to serve it, so it is not icebox-cold.

In a small bowl, toss the tomatoes with the extra-virgin olive oil and the fennel pollen.

When ready to serve, spread the ricotta on the grilled bread and place on a serving plate. Cover with the roasted tomatoes and garnish with crunchy salt.

CO FORNO ROSCIOLI via dei Chiavari, 34 ROMA

pizzette

¼ cup (60 ml) olive oil

3 garlic cloves, peeled

24 ounces (720 ml) bottled tomato passata (I like both Masseria Mirogallo and Mutti)

¾ teaspoon salt

½ teaspoon toasted and ground fennel seed

1 package (about 14 ounces/400 g) all-butter puff pastry (such as Dufour), defrosted in the refrigerator

Crunchy sea salt, to finish

Serves 6 to 8

Pizzette are classic aperitivi snacks, little nibbles that bars give away at the cocktail hour. Honestly, they are not always the greatest—careless kitchens sometimes serve them cold and stiff from the fridge—but even then, they are still kind of irresistible. If you make your own, well, then you've got something so good: the long-cooked tomato merges sweetly with the flaky pastry. Ready-made frozen puff pastry makes this little appetizer completely easy to pull together. Serve them with spritzes or other amari-based cocktails.

In a large, nonreactive saucepan over medium-low, heat the olive oil and garlic for 2 minutes. Pour in the passata and whisk quickly to incorporate. Stir in the salt and fennel seed. Reduce the heat to low and cook, stirring frequently, until thick but spreadable, about 40 minutes. Cool completely (and feel free to store in the refrigerator for a day or two before proceeding).

Heat the oven to 375°F (190°C). Have ready a baking sheet lined with parchment paper.

Remove the puff pastry dough from the package and carefully unfold onto a well-floured surface, trying to not crack the dough.

With a 3-inch (7.5-cm) round cutter, cut the dough into circles, making sure to cut super close so you can get as many circles as possible. Place the rounds on the prepared baking sheet.

With a paring knife, score a circle about ¼ inch (6 mm) inside the perimeter of each round. This will help them puff evenly. Spread about 1 tablespoon of passata onto each round of dough, leaving a ¼-inch (6-mm) border around each circle.

Bake the pizzette until they are puffed and golden brown, about 25 minutes. Cool on a rack to room temperature. Finish with some Maldon or other crunchy sea salt.

chicken liver pâté on crostini with a glass of chianti

1 cup (2 sticks/225 g) unsalted butter, softened, plus 2 tablespoons melted butter for storing

1 medium yellow onion, finely chopped

2 garlic cloves, finely chopped

1 pound (455 g) organic chicken livers, membranes removed

½ teaspoon fresh rosemary, finely chopped

3 tablespoons marsala or brandy

1 teaspoon kosher salt, plus more to taste

¼ cup (60 ml) heavy cream

1 tablespoon dry mustard

½ teaspoon freshly grated nutmeg

⅛ teaspoon cayenne pepper

Crostini, to serve (see page 20)

Serves 10 to 12

Roman cooks have famously made delicious use of the *quinto quarto*, or fifth quarter of butchered animals—that is, the organs that were cheap and readily available to the city's poorer residents. With the right care, such ingredients are extravagant in their own right. Take chicken livers, which I have long loved to blend into a smooth, creamy spread.

There was a time in my life when I'd "steal" things as I left Boat Street, my first restaurant, because I was too tired to cook. I would bring random things home, like a nubbin of cheese and the last bit of this creamy pâté—a classic dish that never came off the menu there. I'd toast some bread to spread it on and sometimes manage to throw together a butter lettuce salad. I loved those quiet moments of unwinding after the mad rush of service. Of course, I'd have a little wine with my food—often the last glass of something we had opened for glass pours, something basic and not too elaborate. I almost think of the Chianti as a condiment to the rich and creamy pâté. Choose your own favorite, but I love the elegant cherry tones of Selvapiana Chianti Rufina.

In a large sauté pan over medium heat, melt half the butter. Add the onion and garlic and cook for 3 minutes, stirring regularly. Add the livers, rosemary, and marsala, season with the 1 teaspoon salt, and cook for about 4 minutes, turning the livers and rearranging them in the pan a few times so each one cooks evenly on both sides. The livers should still be a bit pink in their centers. Remove the pan from the heat and let the livers cool for 5 minutes.

Transfer the sautéed livers to a heavy-duty blender or food processor along with the remaining butter, cream, mustard, nutmeg, and cayenne. Buzz on high speed until completely smooth, 2 to 4 minutes. Spoon into two medium serving bowls.

When fully cool, cover with a thin layer of melted butter, wrap tightly in plastic wrap, and store in the fridge for up to 1 week. You can freeze what you are not going to serve right away, and it will keep for up to 1 month in the freezer. Serve with crostini.

roasted zucchini flowers with ricotta, mint, and lemon peel

Don't let all your zucchinis grow: Grab the prettiest blossoms for a wonderful treat. If you don't have your own squash patch, look—from late spring through most of the summer—for zucchini flowers at farmers' markets or Latin groceries. When we were researching food for Willmott's Ghost, we took a staff tour of Umbria led by my friend Jennifer McIlvaine. One of many great moments was when she served us these. I had had countless fried blossoms before, but it was a revelation to try them stuffed and roasted. Not only is it less messy to make them, but you taste the blossom's peppery brightness more this way. For the filling, make your own ricotta or use a really good basket one, like from Bellwether Farms, or hand-dipped, such as from Calabro Cheese.

2 cups (450 g) whole-milk, basket-molded ricotta
Finely grated zest of 1 lemon (about 1 tablespoon)
2 tablespoons minced mint leaves
Salt and freshly ground black pepper
12 zucchini flowers, stamens (the threadlike pollen parts inside the flower) removed
Extra-virgin olive oil, to drizzle
Crunchy sea salt, to finish

Makes 12 flowers

Heat the oven to 400°F (205°C). Line a half sheet pan with parchment paper and set aside.

In a large bowl, whip the ricotta with a sturdy whisk until it is soft and fluffy. Add the lemon zest, mint, salt, and pepper and whisk to combine.

Hold one blossom in one hand and use the other to spoon it as full as possible with the ricotta filling. Close the end of the flower with a soft twist and place it on the sheet tray. Repeat with the remaining blossoms. Drizzle the flowers liberally with olive oil and season with crunchy salt. Roast for about 10 to 12 minutes, or until they brown and start to get a bit crispy on the edges. Serve while hot!

warm castelluccio lentils on toast with favas, mint, and chèvre

1 cup (200 g) Castelluccio lentils, picked over to remove any tiny pebbles

2 pounds (910 g) fava beans, removed from their pods

1½ cups (270 g) pitted Taggiasca olives, lightly chopped

1 cup (50 g) mint leaves, gently torn into smaller pieces

½ cup (120 ml) really good olive oil, plus more to garnish

Juice and finely grated zest of 1 lemon

½ teaspoon salt, plus more to taste

½ cup (40 g) grated Pecorino Romano

4 slices freshly grilled bread, cooled to room temperature (see page 20 for tips on grilling bread)

6 ounces (170 g) fresh chèvre, at room temperature

Serves 6 to 8

I haven't yet gone to Castelluccio in Norcia, Umbria, but I want to. It's a valley on top of a mountain range where Italy's most famous lentils are grown. The region was very hard hit by the 2016 earthquake, and I hope my love for their signature crop is in some way helping the local economy. The lentils are so lovely: thin-skinned, with no need for soaking, and a nutty, delicate flavor. I like to contrast their earthiness with brightness: fresh green mint and favas, along with some creamy chèvre, so that the whole thing doesn't seem too wholesome. I don't love a mushy lentil, so I cook them like pasta, with heavily salted water, and I test their doneness regularly before draining. They cook very fast, so stay nearby while you are working.

Bring a large pot of salted water to a boil. Drop in the lentils and cook until no longer hard in the center, but still firm, about 20 minutes. Drain and spread on a baking sheet to cool to room temperature.

Prepare a bowl of ice water. Bring a pot of water to a boil and drop in the favas. Let the water come back to a boil and cook for 1 more minute. Scoop the lentils with a slotted spoon and drop into the bowl of ice water. Once chilled, drain, then peel the outer skin off each bean.

In a large bowl, toss together the lentils, favas, olives, and mint. Stir in the olive oil, lemon zest, and some of the lemon juice. Season with salt and then add most of the Pecorino, saving some to garnish the finished toasts. Taste and adjust the seasoning with more lemon juice and salt, as desired. Spread the grilled bread with the soft chèvre, leaving it a bit lumpy and imperfect, but make sure it covers to the edges of each toast.

Top with the lentil salad. Finish with a drizzle more of the olive oil and a generous sprinkle of the Pecorino. Eat right away before the toast gets soggy.

sliced coppa with celery, green olive, and lemon

20 slices very thinly sliced
    coppa
1 cup (about 20 olives/180 g)
    whole Castelvetrano or
    Cerignola green olives,
    pitted
1 cup (20 g) celery leaves, or
    all the celery leaves from
    a bunch, chopped, with a
    few whole leaves set aside,
    to garnish
2 cups (200 g) thinly sliced
    celery stalks from the
    heart, about 6 stalks
1 shallot, thinly sliced
½ cup (120 ml) really good
    olive oil
½ teaspoon crunchy sea salt
1 tablespoon lemon juice
Plenty of freshly ground black
    pepper

Serves 4

When you are swooning at the selection of salumi at a Roman salumeria like La Tradizione, it can be hard to know where to begin. A key distinguishing trait among types of salumi is the manner of processing. With salami, the meat is chopped or ground and put in a casing before fermentation. It's quite different from a whole-muscle product like prosciutto, where the meat is cured without being minced. Another whole-muscle favorite of mine is *coppa*, or *cappocollo*, made from the pork shoulder. I love the contrast between the elegant, slightly spiced meat and the veins of luscious white fat. My favorites have a summery dusting of fennel in their cure. They're delicious on a plate alone, but with a zingy salad of juicy, pale green celery and olives, they become even more fun.

On a serving platter, lay out the coppa, overlapping each slice a bit.

In a bowl, gently toss the olives, celery leaves, celery stalks, shallot, and olive oil together. Add just a bit of the salt and lemon juice at a time, tasting and adjusting the seasonings as necessary.

Pile the salad on top of the coppa in the middle of the platter. Garnish with a bit more celery leaf and a few big grinds of pepper.

no fear of frying

Roman fried delights are almost uncountable: calamari, oxtail meatballs, gnocchi, arancini, artichokes. Crisp, warm, divine! It's not an everyday thing in my house, but it is a favorite way to make party snacks. It's not as hard as you may think. Here's my approach . . .

Don't fry if you are in a hurry: Even though it's a quick method, you want time to set up properly, and you need patience for your fried items to cook evenly without scorching. If you're crabby when you start frying, things aren't likely to go well.

Set up well: You want to have a slotted spoon or a spider (which looks like a wide little basket at the end of a stick). Have a sheet tray ready, topped with either a wire cooling rack or a double layer of paper towels, which you will need to change frequently. Have a thermometer, too. You need a wide heavy pot, filled with at least 3 inches (7.5 cm) of oil. Scorch-resistant neutral oils like grapeseed or sunflower are reliable. You can mix in a little not-too-precious olive oil, too, but don't waste your best stuff on it.

Test: Heat your oil to the desired temperature (refer to your recipe, but 350°F/180°C is a good starting point) and toss in a single drop of batter or a lone *calamaro*, and watch how it responds to the oil. Adjust the temperature a bit up or down if necessary.

Don't crowd the pan: Make sure that each item you are frying has room to swim and bob. It will save you time and materials in the end if you do smaller batches. When the food hits the oil, increase the heat a bit so that the oil can get back to its goal temp quickly. Make sure to reduce the heat when it does.

Salt right away: When the items are cooked, lift them out onto the prepared rack and sprinkle with salt from about 6 inches (15 cm) above to make sure the crust is deliciously seasoned. Don't crowd the cooling rack, or you'll steam the fried food.

semolina-fried squid with lemon aioli

1 pound (455 g) frozen
    cleaned squid, defrosted
About 6 cups (1.4 L) canola or
    sunflower oil, for frying
1 cup (180 g) semolina flour
    (I like Bob's Red Mill
    brand)
Salt
1 batch Lemon Aioli
    (page 338)
Lemon wedges, to serve

Serves 3 to 4

On the shady patio at the Trattoria da Cesare, the Roman restaurant in the quiet Monteverde Nuovo neighborhood, there are many pleasures to be enjoyed. Quite a lot of them are fried. When I ate there, our table was covered with fried treats (see following spread): supple oxtail meatballs, gnocchi, and lovely little paper cones of anchovies, cuttlefish, and of course, calamari. Chef Leonardo Vignoli took me back to his spotless and calm kitchen, where his cooks worked quickly but deliberately. That calm in the kitchen reminded me that even though frying is a quick method, it's best to bring patience to the process—for maximum crispiness, cook in small batches, keep an eye on the temperature of the oil, and be prepared with a landing spot for the just-fried food.

Rinse the squid and drain well. Cut each hood into 3 or 4 slices; keep the tentacle clusters whole.

Have ready a slotted spoon or a spider and a sheet pan topped with either a wire cooling rack or a double layer of paper towels, which you will need to change frequently.

Heat a heavy 4-quart (3.8-L) saucepan or Dutch oven filled with 3 inches (7.5 cm) of canola oil to 350°F (180°C). Adjust the heat to keep the temperature steady.

Place the semolina in a medium bowl. Take a handful of squid and toss in the semolina, then pick up and shake slightly before carefully placing it in the oil, trying to keep the individual pieces separate. The oil will bubble vigorously. Don't add too much squid at one time, or it might overflow. Increase the heat to high while the squid is in the oil.

Cook until the squid is lacy edged and very slightly golden, 1 minute 30 seconds to 1 minute 45 seconds. Lift the squid out of the oil with the spoon or spider and place on the prepared sheet pan. Sprinkle the fried squid with salt.

Reduce the heat a bit and let the oil come back to a steady 350°F (180°C) and repeat, in batches, with the remaining squid.

Serve right away on a platter with the aioli and lemon wedges.

fried salted cod with lemon aioli

One of many Roman fried classics is batter-dipped salt cod, which is deliciously tender and has a distinct, almost olive-like flavor. The truly dried stuff that often comes in a little wooden box is delicious, but it takes a couple of days of soaking to prep. I have a quick version I make by salting fish for a few hours before cooking. The method firms and seasons the fish beautifully but leaves it tender and succulent, too. At Trattoria da Cesare, I learned a great trick for fried fish: When you place it in the hot oil, keep a hold of its tail outside the oil for 30 seconds or so, so that the motion of dropping it in the oil doesn't make the batter slip off. Then gently let it drop into the oil.

In a bowl, whisk together the flour, cornstarch, baking powder, sea salt, white wine, and soda water until almost mixed. A few lumps are OK and preferable to overmixing.

In a heavy 4-quart (3.8-L) pot or Dutch oven, bring 4 inches (10 cm) canola oil to 350°F (180°C) over medium heat. Have a slotted spoon or spider and a baking sheet topped with either a wire cooling rack, or a double layer of paper towels, which you will need to change frequently.

When the oil is ready, dip two or three pieces of fish in the batter and gently place in the oil. Fry for 3 to 4 minutes, making sure to turn the fish once during the frying.

Place on the rack or paper towels to drain, and season with crunchy salt right away. Repeat with the remaining fish. Serve with lemon aioli and lemon wedges.

1 cup (125 g) all-purpose flour
1 cup (130 g) cornstarch
1 teaspoon baking powder
½ teaspoon fine sea salt
1½ cups (360 ml) white wine
½ cup (120 ml) cold soda water
About 6 cups (1.4 liters) canola
    or sunflower oil, for frying
2 pounds (910 g) Homemade
    Salt Cod, rinsed and
    patted dry (page 338)
Crunchy sea salt, to finish
1 batch Lemon Aioli
    (page 338)
Lemon wedges, to serve

Serves 4

Fantastic fritti lunch at Cesare al Casaletto in Rome

crispy zucchini with parmigiano-reggiano, lemon, and mint

3 tablespoons olive oil
1 pound (455 g) zucchini,
 sliced ¾ inch (2 cm) thick
 on the bias
Salt
2 ounces (55 g) Parmigiano-
 Reggiano, ground in a
 blender
1 tablespoon freshly grated
 lemon zest, to garnish
2 tablespoons mint leaves,
 torn
Crunchy sea salt and freshly
 ground black pepper, to
 finish
Really spicy olive oil (optional),
 to finish

Serves 4

This is inspired by the version my mother made with the Parmesan that came in a green can. When I first lived in Rome, I had a roommate who hated zucchini. But I made this dish with squash from the Campo de' Fiori market and even she couldn't resist the chewy cheese crust that coated the zucchini. She loved it then and serves it to her kids to this day. It was one of my earliest culinary conversions! It's truly a summer dish—don't mess around with it until the summer squash are at their peak.

Heat a 10- to 12-inch (25- to 30-cm) heavy iron skillet over medium-high heat. Pour in the olive oil, place the zucchini in a single layer, and season with salt. Reduce the heat to medium and place a little heap of Parmigiano onto each slice and cook, undisturbed, for 2 minutes.

When the bottom of the rounds are browned, use a slender offset spatula to carefully flip each over. Cook for approximately 4 more minutes, until the cheese has browned and crusted. Remove the zucchini to a serving plate, making sure to scrape up the cheese crusts along with the zucchini. Let them cool to room temperature before serving, but after that they are best eaten right away!

Just before serving, grate lemon zest over the zucchini. Garnish with mint leaves, crunchy salt, black pepper, and, if you like, a drizzle of really spicy olive oil.

lamb chops scottadito with roasted potatoes and rosemary

1 cup (240 ml) olive oil, plus more for the grill

2 teaspoons salt, plus more to taste

Lots of freshly ground black pepper, about 2 teaspoons

½ cup (15 g) rosemary leaves, chopped

3 large garlic cloves, chopped

8 generous lamb chops or blade chops, 1½ to 2 inches (4 to 5 cm) thick

1 pound (455 g) small Yukon Gold or butterball potatoes (about 1½ ounces/45 g each)

1 lemon, halved crosswise

Salsa Verde (optional; page 342)

Serves 4

Armando al Pantheon is one of my favorite places in Rome. You would not expect a great restaurant in this tourist-central location—just steps from the Pantheon—but wonderful it is.

Armando serves food that is graceful but matter of fact—like their take on this classic lamb dish. The meat comes out screaming hot and rare, and it is intended to be eaten immediately, thus the name *scottadito*, which means "burnt fingers." You don't need a sauce for these—a lemon is enough. But if you have a few extra minutes, the meat just sings with some delicious salsa verde. This is also equally delicious with lamb blade chops—the lollipops are fancier, but the blade chops make for more interesting char and texture; they are worth the work to eat them. Just keep lots of napkins on hand.

In a small bowl, whisk together the olive oil, salt, pepper, rosemary, and garlic. Set aside ¼ cup (60 ml) and rub the remaining marinade all over the lamb chops. Cover and refrigerate the chops for at least 2 hours (overnight is great).

About an hour before serving, heat the oven to 425°F (220°C) and remove the chops from the refrigerator. Toss the potatoes with the reserved marinade and place in a baking dish. Roast the potatoes until golden brown and tender, about 30 minutes.

Prepare a charcoal grill by heating until the flames die away and the coals are ashed over. Spread the coals, replace the grate, and wait for the grate to heat up, about 10 minutes. Give the grate a good scraping with a brush once hot. Soak a piece of paper towel with olive oil and, using tongs, rub it on the grate to thoroughly coat.

Lift the lamb chops out of the marinade and grill over medium-high heat for about 4 minutes per side, until browned and the fat is cooked but the interiors are still rare. Dip the cut sides of the lemon in the marinade and place on the grill to cook alongside the lamb. The lemons are ready when well charred. Serve the lamb with the lemon, potatoes, and, if desired, the salsa verde.

eggplant parmigiano

3 pounds (1.4 kg) eggplant
(about 3 large)

Kosher salt

All-purpose flour, to dust

1 to 1½ cups (250 to 375 ml)
olive oil, plus more for the
casserole dish

Freshly ground black pepper

1 pound (455 g) low-moisture
mozzarella, shredded

4 cups (1 L) Tomato Sauce
(page 343)

4 ounces (115 g) Parmigiano-
Reggiano cheese, grated,
plus more for serving

Serves 8 to 10

Great baked vegetable casseroles, like this one, feed crowds so well. This one is inspired by two sources: my beloved Armando al Pantheon, which has a fab version, and Elizabeth David, the writer who stoked the British passion for Italian eating. She had a breezy style to her recipes, even if they can be irritatingly vague. So here I've tried to be a little more helpful in my instructions, while hoping you still find the recipe charming and approachable!

Peel the eggplant and cut it lengthwise into ¼-inch (6-mm) slices, stem to bottom. Salt the slices lightly on both sides and lay them in a colander to drain for 1½ hours.

Have ready either a wire cooling rack or a double layer of paper towels, which you will need to change frequently.

Using a paper towel, press each slice of the eggplant to absorb surface moisture and remove any large chunks of salt. Dust each slice with flour on both sides. Heat ¼ inch (6 mm) of oil in a large, cast-iron skillet over high heat. Lay a few eggplant slices in the pan, making sure they do not overlap, and fry until golden brown on both sides, about 45 to 50 seconds on each side. When cooked, remove each slice to the cooling rack to drain. Using a wad of paper towels, wipe out the pan, making sure to clear off any burnt bits. Pour in another ¼ inch (6 mm) of oil and repeat until all the slices are fried.

Heat the oven to 350°F (180°C). To assemble, rub the sides of a 3-quart (3-L) oval casserole dish with olive oil. Place one layer of the cooked eggplant in the dish. Season with a few grinds of pepper and sprinkle with mozzarella and a scoop of tomato sauce (remembering that the cheese and the sauce is to be distributed over five or six layers). Continue layering with all the remaining eggplant, finishing with a final layer of mozzarella and tomato sauce. Cover the casserole with the grated Parmigiano. Bake for 1½ hours, covering with foil around halfway through, when the casserole is a little browned and burbling with juices.

The casserole can be served immediately, but I prefer it chilled overnight and then reheated till super crispy on top and bubbling up the sides, about 45 minutes. Top with more freshly grated Parmigiano just before serving.

The market Campo de' Fiori, Rome

roman mercati

It was late summer when I arrived for that semester in Rome, and hot as hell, but I loved to walk and walk and walk. Every day on my way to school, I would walk through the Piazza Navona to the Campo de' Fiori, the huge market square that stood right in front of the UW Center in the Palazzo Pio. I'd stroll past butchers, bakeries, pasta shops, and little *alimentari* (grocery stores) along the way, getting more excited as I passed more vendors. Sometimes, I would stop. I learned that curiosity was often rewarded with a sample, like the refrigerated cheese truck guy who would give me a little bite of something when I started asking questions. Of course, more often than not, I then bought a little sliver of aged provolone from him for a cheap lunch.

At the Campo de' Fiori itself, the stalls in the square were piled high with peppers and tomatoes and gleaming summer squash. One day, I spotted a couple with a small cart covered in mountains of what I now know were porcinis. I was so curious about the big mushrooms, and in my mediocre Italian I asked for four. One of the merchants, who looked like she, too, had sprung up from the forest floor, tallied them up, and it took me a moment to realize that she was asking for something close to $50. Of course, I couldn't afford that. But I did hand her the lira for a single porcini. I roasted it and ate it slowly, thrilled at the sweet taste and my successful transaction. Now I know we have similar boletes in the woods of Washington State, and though I can afford more of them these days, I still can't get enough.

Those months in Rome completely opened my eyes to uncomplicated food made from good ingredients, from costly mushrooms to the simplest hunk of good bread. To this day, when I get to a new city, the thing I want to do is go through a market, to see the things that are just begging to be brought home and cooked that very day.

That said, I don't really shop at the Campo de' Fiori when I visit Rome anymore, as it is now heavy on rainbow-colored pasta and flavored olive oils in bottles the shape of Italy. There is still some produce to be had, but as I get to know Rome better, I have made a point to get out to some of the other neighborhoods to shop instead.

roman mercati (continued)

One great place for food is the Mercato Trionfale. It's ugly—kind of like a mall from the late seventies—but there is shade, parking, and room to wander around. Many of the customers are pensioners who give stall owners a hard time if their produce is not up to snuff, so by and large, the artichokes are plump, the tomatoes ripe and heavy, and any withered shelling beans are banished to the waste heap.

The other great thing about the Trionfale market is that it's across the way from two of Rome's greatest gastronomic treasures. First, there's La Tradizione, the specialty food store to the most exalted Romans (and likely the high-ranking Vatican officials who live right nearby). Every surface is covered with glorious food. Salumi hangs from the ceiling and in the deli cases. One case holds soft-rind cheeses; another, a staircase of aged Pecorino big enough for a toddler to climb. The prepared foods are lovely, too: marinated peppers, eggplant, olives, fish—you name it. This place is where you would assemble an antipasto plate for the gods.

Just across the way is another celebrated space—the original Pizzarium Bonci, where Gabriele Bonci renewed the glorious Roman tradition of pizza al taglio by mastering a crisp-chewy crust and topping it with creative combinations of carefully sourced ingredients. You'll find pizza topped with chickpea paste and bitter greens, or eggplant and mozzarella. I've borrowed some of his ideas for my own restaurant Willmott's Ghost, like a pizza topped with olive-oily crushed potatoes. Divine.

Almost impossible to choose at Pizzarium Bonci—here, just a few of the options (counterclockwise from middle left): ricotta, onions, and arugula; mozzarella and roasted green peppers; eggplant with burrata; and chickpea puree and mortadella.

paris

apéritifs, vermouth, and tartines

Paris is the place I can always dip into to restore my creativity. There are some timeless pleasures, of course, like knowing that I can always find great bread, great wine, and great cheese. I'll walk and walk and walk near my favorite spots, taking in the soothing rhythm of the arcades at the Place des Vosges, the graceful allées at the Jardin du Luxembourg, and the intimate charm of the Musée Picasso in the Marais. I'll almost always make time to wander through the extraordinary President Wilson farmers' market, gaping at the mountains of radishes, forests of sunflowers, and icy mounds of silvery fish. I regularly check in for a glass at Le Baron Rouge, an old favorite wine bar that's reliably packed and reliably fun.

But for every bit of Paris that I can count on, there are almost as many changes to take in—that's the beauty of it. Paris is the place where young people from around the world come to prove themselves in the worlds of fashion, design, and food, and that vitality is so much a part of every trip to Paris for me.

Cave de Belleville, Paris

paris

I might discover a new wine, or an appealing way to serve cheese, or remember that I really like an ingredient that I'd neglected for a while.

It's the casual world of wine bars—especially in the neighborhoods like the upper Marais and Belleville, and often in the hands of expatriate chefs—where things shift most quickly. The great classics of casual French food are met with grace notes from around the world, like Korean *gochujang*, Spanish *ajo blanco*, and jewel-bright slices of Floridian limequat. The sacred art of French baking is being reframed with whole grains and sourdough cultures, even in the croissants!

The hippie factor is high in the new Paris—natural wines dominate youthful wine bars these days—and the shift in focus means that even old familiars like chardonnay and pinot noir can startle you with new flavors. No longer are bar menus completely focused on meat and cheese (though don't worry, you can always find good charcuterie), they also have surprisingly robust selections of vegetables and seafood. The music is likely to be loud; the crowd even louder.

It's not always something specific that I take home from Paris: It's more a commitment to the casual way that Parisians enjoy their *apéro* hour. When I get back, I want to keep that chic and effortless spirit going. If I'm not serving Champagne or a Beaujolais, I'll mix an easy vermouth cocktail. To go with that, I'll put together a super-rustic charcuterie board or improvise some tartines (open-faced sandwiches), putting a jar full of knives on the table like they do in the wine bars, so that people can cut off a nibble for themselves. I'll often steam some shellfish (maybe with another glug of that vermouth). And there is always plenty of bread and good butter to fill in the corners.

Of course, you can get the fanciest food in the world in Paris, but this chapter is here to convince you that you can steal a little of that slouchy wine-bar style for your own home.

lillet martini

4 ounces (120 ml) dry gin
2 ounces (60 ml) vodka
1½ ounces (45 ml) Lillet
1 lemon, for peeling

Makes 2 cocktails

This drink is a classic and is super easy to make. We took to serving it when we first added cocktails at the new Boat Street, where I had my first bar. I wanted drinks that were delicious but not too complicated to make. This drink is so minimal that it calls out to be served up in a pretty little glass. If I make one for myself, and I don't drink it fast enough (and I rarely drink cocktails fast), I'll float an ice cube in it for a minute, and then remove it to achieve just the right chill. I am definitely Goldilocks when it comes to my cocktails.

Chill two glasses by filling with ice. In a mixing glass filled with ice, add the gin, vodka, and Lillet and stir. Stir some more, so much so that the outside of your mixing glass frosts up. Dump the ice from the glasses, and strain the gin mixture into them. Peel a 2-inch (5-cm) strip of lemon for each drink and squeeze over the glass, releasing the lemon oils. You will smell it—it's heavenly. Run the peel over the edge of the glass and float the peel onto each cocktail. Drink fast, or add an ice cube later like I do.

Byrrh Vermouth Spritz

the perfect vermouth

Vermouth is the ideal way to wade into bitter, complex spirits without getting whomped on the head with medicinal flavors (those are fun, too, but not necessarily for newcomers). Vermouth is wine that has been blended with aromatics and spirits, and it has three basic profiles: red (used in Manhattans and negronis), white (terrific on its own or in a highball), and dry (used in martinis). I like to give vermouth a chance to be the star attraction, not just the accent to another spirit, and so here I combine two of those styles—aromatic white vermouth and a more austere dry—for a luscious and refreshing drink.

3 ounces (90 ml) dry vermouth, such as Dolin Dry
3 ounces (90 ml) white vermouth, such as Dolin Bianco
2 strips orange zest

Makes 2 cocktails

Place a large ice cube in each of two cocktail glasses. Pour equal amounts of each vermouth into each glass, and stir. Place the orange zest in each glass and serve.

byrrh vermouth spritz

Byrrh is a funky old aperitif—first produced in 1866—with notes of coffee, orange peel, and a bit of quinine's distinct bitterness. It's a warmer flavor palate than some other aperitifs, so I like it in this drink with the licorice bite of pastis. It's a little crazy, but sometimes crazy works.

2 ounces (60 ml) Byrrh
1½ ounces (45 ml) Contratto Americano Rosso
1 ounce (30 ml) pastis
Crémant de Bourgogne or other dry sparkling wine, to top
Lemon slices, to garnish
Edible flowers, such as feverfew (optional)

Makes 2 cocktails

Fill two tall glasses three-quarters of the way with ice. Divide the Byrrh, Contratto, and pastis evenly between both glasses and stir. Top each glass with crémant and stir, then garnish with the lemon slices and flowers, if using.

le boat street

4 ounces (120 ml) Pineau des
    Charentes Blanc
Dash of Angostura bitters
1 ounce (30 ml) lemon juice
2 strips lemon zest, trimmed
    into pointed ribbons
Crémant de Bourgogne or
    other dry sparkling wine,
    to top

Makes 2 cocktails

Here's a fancy-tasting cocktail from Boat Street's bar that's deceptively simple to make. It's built on sparkling wine and round, luscious Pineau des Charentes Blanc. For years this has been one of my favorite fortified wines from France for cocktails. I love the stone fruit sweetness balanced with great acidity. You can prepare the Pineau part for several drinks all at once and then just pour in the sparkling wine to finish. One sweet, slightly fussy detail makes it feel special: an extra-pretty lemon twist to hang in each glass.

In a cocktail shaker filled with ice, shake the Pineau des Charantes, bitters, and lemon juice.

Rub the rims of two Champagne flutes with the lemon zest. Strain the mixture into the flutes, and then top with the sparkling wine. Place a strip of lemon zest in each glass.

l'après swim

3 ounces (90 ml) pastis
1 ounce (30 ml) lemon juice
Crémant de Bourgogne or
    other dry sparkling wine,
    to top
Geranium sprig or another
    edible flower, to garnish

Makes 2 cocktails

Stop me before I buy another vintage pastis water bottle! I've always been fascinated by the classic French afternoon ritual of drinking the licorice-flavored liqueur, which comes in a glass of ice, and into which you stir water to dilute to your taste. The whole thing turns dramatically cloudy. If I am at a café, I'll peek around to see just what ratio of pastis to water the regulars take.

This drink, just a hair more complex than the classic dilution method, is also a perfect afternoon refreshment, perhaps after a day at the beach. Lemon juice lightens up the sheer black-jellybean licorice of the pastis. And the sparkling wine, well, who doesn't smile when a drink is topped off with bubbles?

In a cocktail pitcher filled with crushed ice (see page 28 for a method of preparing this), stir the pastis and lemon juice together.

Fill two cocktail glasses three-quarters of the way with crushed ice, then strain the cocktail over. Top with sparkling wine and garnish with a geranium sprig.

L'Après Swim

After lunch in Paris at Le Baratin

wine for the people!

Beer is surprisingly chic in Paris now, and that's fine, but really, it's hard to not order wine when I am there. I have two basic modes when I am drinking in Paris: "Champagne" and "not Champagne."

Unlike many spots in the United States, it is easy to get a good glass of Champagne in my favorite Paris wine bars, and I love the instant lift that comes with a glass of bubbling wine, especially if it can be had at lunchtime. Champagne is a great wine to have with food, from potato chips, which are beloved at Paris wine bars, to rather more elegant oysters and beef tartare. I look for interesting grower Champagnes, like the minerally *blanc de blancs* from Jacques Lassaigne or Marie-Courtin's *cuvée* Pinot Noirs.

As for "not Champagne," you can try every kind of wine under the sun, and I try to open my eyes to old favorites and new discoveries alike. Right now, natural wine bars are completely dominating the wine scene in Paris (and frankly they are setting the tone in most big European cities).

Natural wine is a bit under-defined and can lead you down many paths. The basic gist is a good one: Start with organic or biodynamic viniculture, and then add as little as possible to get to wine. That means things like picking grapes by hand, maybe leaving them on the stem, being choosy about how they are pressed (if they are pressed at all), avoiding lab-cultured yeasts, or not filtering or fining wines to clarify them. And many natural wines are proudly *sans sufs* ("without sulfites"), meaning the preservative sulfur dioxide is not added to curtail bacterial action in the bottle. (There are still natural sulfates in wine though, so it's not quite as "sans" as it sounds.)

Natural wines don't taste one way—all that microbial action means, in fact, that there is more variety among natural wines in a single category, even from a single maker, than we have grown used to with conventional wines. Places like Beaujolais have been practicing very low-intervention winemaking for decades, and its winemakers are making their own natural classics. Natural wine in the hands of a careless winemaker is less compelling, and without chemical or physical interventions, their errors in winemaking aren't covered up by anything.

The key to finding a natural wine to love is the same as when you choose any wine: Ask questions and revisit places that let you take a little taste before committing to a glass. The more you talk with your server, the more you are likely to taste something you like. The thing I love about La Buvette or Au Passage or Le Grand Bain is that the servers are interested in helping you find something you love. When I go to a wine bar with a natural focus, I ask for more "classic" wines, and ask not to be served wines that are "cidery," "extreme," or even "mousy." There are plenty of people who appreciate wines with those qualities, but I'm not one of them. When you do hit upon a beautifully crafted natural wine, say a chardonnay from Fanny Sabre or Athénaïs de Béru, it can make you notice exciting new tones in a beloved old grape.

wine for the people! *(continued)*

Like I said, when I am in Paris, I most often drink wine, but when I am home and thinking of Paris, that's a different matter—then I often lean on mixed drinks built on vermouths and other softer fortified wines, which have a bitter element but are not as punchy as some of the spirited Italian bitters. Besides wine, vermouth may be my favorite thing to drink. It's great on its own, and a fantastic shortcut to a two- or three-ingredient cocktail (my kind of cocktail!), because it brings complexity without having to do too much measuring, muddling, zesting, or shaking. It's perfectly fine to have a vermouth on the rocks with a twist and call it a day; just remember to keep that open bottle in the fridge, not your cupboard, and drink it within about two months of opening. And all styles of vermouth are a fantastic addition to the cooking pantry, too—I'll often start cooking with them when they have been opened for more than a month and are losing freshness. Try a splash of dry Dolin vermouth in steamed shellfish or a bit of the gorgeous La Quintinye Rouge vermouth to deglaze a sautéed chicken dish.

radishes and whipped basil butter

Au Passage is cramped and noisy and no longer undiscovered, but this natural wine bar still stands out: The servers are funky and helpful (not always a given in Paris!), the room is bubbling with conversation, and the food has a delicious clarity, even when you're eating a classic. Last time I was there, I ordered radishes and butter—a dish I've seen and served one thousand times before—but the butter was silky and infused with herbs. We lapped it up, and I quickly got to thinking about how to make my own version. Here it is. You can make and cool the basil puree a few hours before serving, but once you've whipped the butter, do not put it in the fridge before serving if you want this to be soft and supple enough to dip your radishes into. After your party, any remaining butter can be refrigerated and used for other dishes, such as steamed clams, roasted veggies, or just spread on toast.

2 cups (80 g) packed basil leaves
2 teaspoons olive oil, plus more to drizzle
1 pound (455 g) unsalted butter, at room temperature
2 teaspoons finely grated lemon zest
Salt
2 bunches radishes, washed, stems trimmed to leave a ½-inch (12-mm) stem at top

Serves 4 to 6

Have ready a medium bowl of ice water. Bring a medium saucepan of salted water to a boil. Submerge the basil leaves in the water and blanch just until the leaves turn bright green and transparent, about 15 seconds. Plunge into the ice bath and cool.

When cool, remove the basil from the water and squeeze dry. Set aside on a towel to continue to dry. When fully dry, place the basil in a blender with ¼ cup (60 ml) water and the olive oil and blend for 2 minutes. Pour the basil puree through a fine-mesh strainer set over a bowl.

In a stand mixer fitted with the paddle attachment, or using a hand mixer, whip the butter for 2 to 3 minutes, until it is soft and fluffy. Slowly add the strained basil puree to the whipped butter. Continue to whip on low until the basil has been incorporated. Fold in the lemon zest and season with salt.

Season the radishes lightly with salt and a drizzle of olive oil and place on a serving platter next to a generous schmear of whipped butter. Store extra butter in the refrigerator for a couple of days or the freezer for 2 months.

tarama and potato chips

1¼ packed cups (145 g) white or sourdough bread, torn into 1-inch (2.5-cm) pieces (about 4 slices; remove the crusts if it's a chewy loaf)
4 ounces (120 g) salmon eggs
1 garlic clove, chopped
2 tablespoons lemon juice
½ cup (120 ml) olive oil
1 teaspoon salt, plus more if needed
Potato chips (see page 304 to make your own, or pick a favorite brand), to serve

Serves 4 to 6

Tarama, short for *taramasalata*, is Greek in origin, but it's completely at home on the bar menus of Paris: You'll find it at Martin, Clamato, even in the grocery store. It's a spread traditionally made with bread and cod or carp roe, but here in the Pacific Northwest, I can get salty cured salmon roe, or *ikura*, in great shape and without preservatives, so I use that. The texture of the tarama will vary with the bread you use; you can always add a bit more water and/or oil if the mixture is too thick.

Dampen the bread with a couple tablespoons of water to soften, and let it sit for 10 minutes.

In a blender, combine ¼ cup (60 ml) water with the bread, salmon eggs, garlic, lemon juice, olive oil, and salt. Blend until smooth. Taste and adjust the salt, if necessary. The tarama can be stored in the refrigerator for up to 1 day before serving. Serve with the chips.

big white beans, agrumato oil, and black pepper

1 pound (455 g) dried large
   white beans like gigante
   or corona beans (seek out
   very fresh dried beans,
   like those from Rancho
   Gordo)
3½ teaspoons salt
1 bay leaf
½ whole yellow onion
Freshly ground black pepper
½ cup (125 ml) agrumato oil
   (olive oil pressed with
   lemon peels)
Finely grated lemon zest, to
   garnish

Serves 4

La Buvette, Camille Fourmont's tiny little wine bar in a former cheese shop in the 11th, set a fire—in Paris and on Instagram—with its tiny tiled space, its incredible connections to natural winemakers, and its limited but irresistible food offerings. From a restaurateur's standpoint, I'm just so impressed with the way she and her staff keep the crowds happy in such a small space—it's so calm and pleasant to be there, and the locals pop in to take home a bottle even as travelers from around the world wait for their chance to photograph the handwritten menu. Along with good charcuterie from local suppliers like Le Repaire de Cartouche, La Buvette serves perfect grazing food, including a beautiful pile of big, plump white beans topped with olive oil and lemon zest. Here's my tribute, using olive oil that has been pressed with lemon peels to boost the lemon factor.

In a large container, cover the beans with three times the volume of water as the beans themselves. Stir in 1 teaspoon salt and let soak for 14 to 16 hours, discarding any beans that are still floating and very hard.

Drain the beans, place them in a large pot with two times their volume of water, and stir in 1 teaspoon salt. Add the bay leaf and onion. Bring to a boil, then reduce the heat to a gentle simmer for 60 to 90 minutes, until the beans are completely cooked and not white at their centers, stirring often. Remove any beans that still look chalky and white after cooking.

When cooked through, drain (keep the liquid) and cool the beans in a shallow pan. You can cook the beans ahead of time and store them in their liquid in the fridge for up to 1 week. Let the beans come to room temperature before serving.

Pile the drained beans in a low bowl or platter and season them with the remaining salt, lots of black pepper, and the agrumato oil. Top with a shower of freshly grated zest. This is best eaten right away.

currant and hazelnut anchoïade with crudités

Underneath the huge trees of the Boulevard du Temple, you might wonder what the enormous crowd is for: row after row of people milling around on the sidewalk, then more seated in a covered patio, and in the back, a bar, too. Young Parisiennes, in high-waisted jeans and eighties-style blazers, cluster around. Saucisse, the portly wiener dog, patrols the space, though he isn't very social and will retreat behind the bar—in what was apparently once a betting parlor—when things get too crowded. This is Martin, and unlike many cool places in Paris that are only big enough for a handful of people, it's expansive (but packed!). The crowds are here for cheap beer, groovy natural wines, and beyond. The chalkboard menu is familiar to any Paris visitor, but there is a little difference: There are lots and lots of vegetables, like little plates with beets, artichokes, and asparagus, although to be sure, when I ate there, I had a huge hunk of pork belly, too. Owner Loïc Martin, who runs the happening place with unflappable warmth, told us that most of the vegetables come from the restaurant's own farm. In that spirit, here's a gutsy dip that you can pair with favorite fresh veggies from your own garden, or someone else's, and change them around with the seasons. You could also toss any leftover *anchoïade* with spaghetti for a late-night dinner.

15 anchovy fillets
3 garlic cloves, peeled
¼ cup (45 g) dried currants, soaked for 15 minutes in warm water, then drained
½ cup (70 g) toasted hazelnuts
¾ cup (180 ml) olive oil, plus more to taste
2 tablespoons lemon juice, plus more to taste
Zest of 1 lemon
1 cup (100 g) roughly chopped Italian parsley leaves
Salt
¼ teaspoon chile flakes
Fresh and delightful seasonal vegetables, cut into snackable sizes

Serves 4 to 6

In a food processor, combine the anchovies, garlic, currants, hazelnuts, olive oil, lemon juice and zest, parsley, salt, and chile flakes. Pulse a few times to combine, and then blend into a coarse puree, about 1 minute. Taste and adjust the seasoning with additional salt, olive oil, and/or lemon juice. Serve with the vegetables. Store the anchoïade 1 day in the fridge.

fried sardines, sunflower tarator, and lemon

1 cup (115 g) packed 1-inch (2.5-cm) white bread chunks

1½ cups (210 g) toasted sunflower seeds

2 garlic cloves, smashed

1 teaspoon salt

1 tablespoon lemon juice

1½ cups (360 ml) olive oil

2 (4.2-ounce/120-g) cans high-quality sardines, such as Matiz, drained

Lemon wedges, to serve

Serves 4

Marinated, fried, or grilled, the sardines of Paris are plentiful and delicious. I especially love the airy, batter-fried sardines with a thick, garlicky sauce at Le Saint Sébastien. They are showered in yellow broccoli flowers as a very-of-the-moment way to dress up the otherwise beige dish. The sardines of the Pacific Northwest would be very good, too, if we could get them in the fish market with any consistency. But they are hard to find, and so I usually satisfy my cravings with excellent tinned fish. They are lovely with my own thick, garlicky sauce: a sunflower seed variation on the Turkish bread-and-walnut condiment *tarator*.

In a small bowl, toss the bread with about ¼ cup (60 ml) water and let stand for 10 minutes. Remove the bread from the bowl, squeeze out any excess water, and set the bread aside.

In a blender, pulse the sunflower seeds until coarsely chopped. Add the softened bread, garlic, salt, and lemon juice and process for 15 seconds to mix. With the motor running, gradually pour the olive oil into the blender in a thin stream. Blend thoroughly to create a smooth emulsion.

Spread about half the tarator on a serving plate and keep it near the stove.

Heat a grill pan or cast-iron skillet over medium-high heat. Lay in the sardines and cook for about 2 minutes. Carefully flip and cook for about 2 more minutes. Turn off the heat and remove with a slotted spatula, piling them high on the tarator-prepared plate. The sardines are fragile, so be careful if you want them to stay whole. Drizzle with olive oil and serve with wedges of lemon. Any extra tarator can be refrigerated for up to a week and can be served as a dip with crudités.

the art of tartines

One of the undersung treats of French cuisine is the tartine—the open-faced sandwich you can find at bars and bakeries, and of course, in French homes, too.

Tartines are totally unprepossessing—when I make one at home, I'm often using leftovers. But they have a certain order to them, too.

The rules of tartines are pretty simple: Good bread is the first, of course. Tartines are best made with a *pain au levain*, with a light sourdough touch and an earthy bit of whole grain. If you can't find that, you could work with a not-too-holey white sourdough. It is also ideal if the bread slice is long and paddle-shaped: Somehow a slice of square sandwich bread isn't right, conceptually. If you use a baguette, slice at a strong diagonal to get an oblong piece. In France, your tartine bread will not necessarily be toasted, but personally, I usually like to toast before spreading.

Then there is the spreading part—*tartiner* means "to spread," after all. I typically make sure there's plenty of butter on a tartine, though you could argue against it if you are making a chèvre tartine, for example. But there's nothing wrong with butter *and* chèvre!

Then, the main affair, whether it is cheese or salami or ham or pâté. The key here is to evenly distribute the ingredient. If you're talking salami, deal the slices evenly across the whole face of the bread slice. If you are spreading chicken liver mousse, make sure it goes all the way to the edge of the bread. The layer shouldn't be too thick, causing the bread to flop when you pick it up, nor should it be too skimpy.

And finally, the garnish. It can be as simple as a bit of crunchy salt and pepper, or something more elaborate. As rustic as tartines are, they often have the wink of something cheerful to finish them: a few herbs, an olive here or there, or a cross-sectioned cornichon.

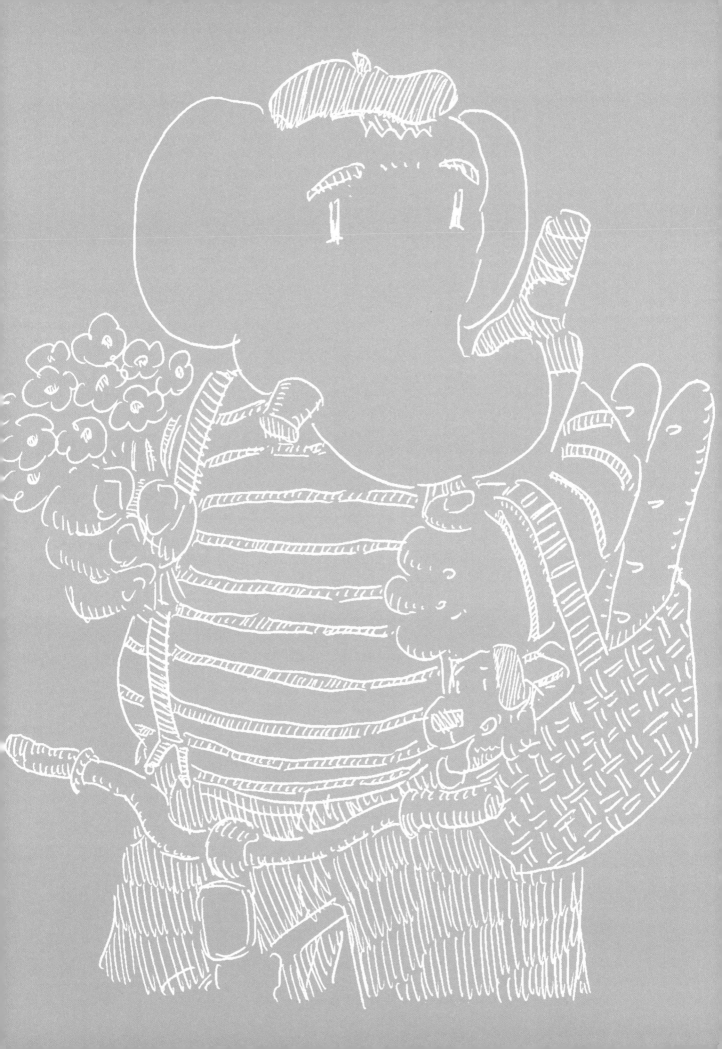

fresh chèvre tartine with shredded carrots, currants, and dukkah

¼ cup (45 g) dried currants

⅓ cup (75 ml) warm water

4 carrots, trimmed, peeled, and shredded

Finely grated zest from 2 limes

4 tablespoons (60 ml) lime juice (about 2 limes)

½ cup (120 ml) olive oil, plus more to garnish

½ cup (75 g) dukkah, plus more to garnish

Salt and freshly ground black pepper (optional)

1 cup (100 g) whole Italian parsley leaves

6 ounces (170 g) fresh goat cheese, at room temperature

4 slices sourdough bread, sliced ¾ inch (2 cm) thick, grilled (see page 20 for notes on grilling bread)

Serves 4 to 8

One of the classic French deli salads is a carrot salad. It's grandma food, and often a little under-seasoned, but I still love the texture and the color that it adds to a plate. Here's my tribute in tartine form, where I add the sharp bite of fresh chèvre beneath the carrots, and a little *dukkah*, the Egyptian-inspired spice and nut blend, on top to give texture and extra complexity.

In a small bowl, cover the currants with the warm water. Let sit for at least 10 minutes.

Drain the currants. In a medium bowl, combine the currants, carrots, lime zest, lime juice, olive oil, and dukkah. Taste and season with salt and pepper, if desired. Toss in the parsley leaves.

Generously spread some goat cheese on each toast. Top with a lofty pile of the carrot mixture. Garnish with extra dukkah and a drizzle of olive oil.

roast beef tartines for a crowd

Bar de la Croix Rouge, the trusty old wine bar in the 6th arrondissement, is a great place to appreciate the simplicity of a good tartine. It's been a few years, but I can still picture the pink beef, well-seasoned and placed evenly on a slice of toasted levain bread and cut crosswise into thin strips. So simple, but so satisfying. Back at home, I love to add a little dab of horseradish cream instead of the Dijon that sits on most Parisian bistro tables. Roast beef is one of those dishes that's hard to do in small batches—you can have some for dinner one night and then make tartines for a later meal; or use the whole roast to make a whole bunch of tartines for your next gathering. Note that the beef needs time to marinate and to cool—it's not quite a spontaneous dish.

In a medium bowl, whisk together the olive oil, black pepper, salt, and thyme. Rub all over the sirloin, cover well, and refrigerate overnight.

Heat the oven to 325°F (170°C). Pull the roast from the refrigerator, place it on a sturdy baking sheet, and let it sit at room temperature for 1 hour. Roast the beef for 75 to 90 minutes, or until a thermometer inserted into the deepest part of the roast reads 120°F (50°C) for a rosy rare interior. Remove the meat from the oven and cover with aluminum foil; the temperature will continue to rise for about 20 minutes. Let it cool entirely, placing it in the refrigerator once at room temperature, if you are finishing the tartines the next day.

When you are ready to serve, remove the strings on the roast and slice as thinly as possible, aiming for paper-thin ruffles.

Spread a liberal layer of the horseradish cream on each piece of bread. Arrange a pretty pile of beef slices atop the cream, drizzle with olive oil, and sprinkle with crunchy salt and a few grinds of black pepper.

¼ cup (60 ml) olive oil, plus more for drizzling

2 teaspoons freshly ground black pepper, plus more to garnish

2 tablespoons kosher salt

3 tablespoons minced thyme leaves

5 pounds (2.3 kg) top sirloin roast, trimmed and tied

1 batch Horseradish Cream (page 338)

1 slice of grilled sourdough bread per person (see page 20 for tips on toasting)

Olive oil, to toast sourdough and garnish

Crunchy sea salt, to finish

Serves up to 12 people

beef tartare, oyster aioli, pickled baby onions, and potato chips

8 ounces (225 g) top sirloin, minced

¼ cup (60 ml) really good olive oil, plus more to finish

2 teaspoons lemon juice

3 dashes hot sauce

2 tablespoons minced shallot (about 1 medium shallot)

1 tablespoon minced capers, preferably salt-packed, rinsed and soaked 10 minutes, drained

Salt and freshly ground black pepper

Oyster Aioli (page 339)

Pickled Onions, to serve (page 341)

1 tablespoon chives, cut into ½-inch (12-mm) matchsticks, to serve (optional)

Potato chips (see page 304 to make your own, or pick a favorite brand), to serve

Serves 4

You know you're living the life when you're eating beef tartare and frites at Brasserie Lipp (a 140-year-old restaurant in the 6th arrondissement) and you spy Mick Jagger at the table next to you, like I did several years ago. Decadence in every direction! I love tartare so much, and it's a lot easier to make than you might think. Just conspire with a good butcher for meat you trust. And before you cut it up, let it sit in the freezer for an hour, to make it easy to cut into tiny bits.

In a medium bowl, combine the sirloin, olive oil, lemon juice, hot sauce, shallot, capers, salt, and pepper.

Spoon the aioli in a nice ring around the center of a chilled serving plate. Pile the tartare up in the middle of the ring, making sure to keep some of the aioli peeking out the side. Place the pickled onions and chopped chives around the border and drizzle generously with good olive oil. Serve with potato chips.

barely cooked oysters with saffron and vermouth cream

2 tablespoons olive oil

2 tablespoons unsalted butter

2 large leeks, white and light green parts only, washed and sliced ¼ inch (6 mm) thick

1½ cups (360 ml) heavy cream

1½ teaspoons freshly squeezed lemon juice, plus more to taste

Pinch of saffron

⅓ cup (75 ml) dry vermouth

12 oysters, shucked, with ¼ cup (60 ml) oyster liquor strained and reserved

Salt

Pinch of cayenne pepper

Chives and thyme leaves, to garnish

Crunchy sea salt, to finish

4 slices sourdough bread, grilled (see page 20 for tips on grilling bread)

Serves 4

Keeping vermouth in the fridge isn't just great for impromptu cocktails—it's an easy way to add a little mystery and depth to saucy dishes like this elegant little oyster stew. Cooking oysters is all about timing. Before adding the oysters, you can get everything else cooked, but wait until you are ready to serve the stew before slipping the oysters into the creamy broth. Have warm bowls ready and crusty bread on hand, and serve the oysters promptly, just as soon as they have plumped.

In a wide, nonreactive saucepan over medium-high, heat the olive oil and butter. Once the butter is melted, add the leeks and sweat for about 4 minutes. Reduce the heat to medium and add the cream, lemon juice, saffron, vermouth, and oyster liquor. Simmer for 5 to 6 minutes, until the mixture thickens and coats the back of a spoon.

Increase the heat back to medium-high, add the oysters, and simmer for another 4 to 5 minutes. They are ready when the edges ruffle up and their bellies are just firm to the touch. Taste and add salt, cayenne, and more lemon juice, if desired.

Serve warm in a bowl with chives, thyme, and crunchy salt as garnish. Have the grilled bread ready on the side.

charcuterie with france in mind

There's a lot of general overlap between French and Italian charcuterie, but there are a few serving details that can push things in a more French direction. As much as I like a paper-thin slice of delicate salami, I also love the chunky way some French wine bars, like Le Café de la Nouvelle Mairie, serve theirs. So, when I'm thinking of Paris and putting together a charcuterie board, I often prefer thick slices of salami with unruly chunks of fat in it.

I'll arrange it on a plate or a cutting board, drizzle some olive oil on it, and serve it with softened, salted French butter. Butter with cured meats is just the best. Look for imported, cultured French butter that has a tanginess to it. The absolute dreamiest is Bordier butter, but for now, it's almost impossible to buy here. Good thing there are other good options, like Le Meunier.

Slightly sour bread, whether it is in a boule or a baguette form, also makes a charcuterie moment feel more French. I crave that sharp, crackly crust and an airy but chewy interior. To that point, don't forget the classic trick to recrisp crusty bread on the second day: Dampen the outside of a loaf and throw it in an oven at 325°F (170°C) for 10 minutes or so (keeping a careful eye not to burn it).

If I'm not serving salami, I still keep the same chunky aesthetic in mind: Maybe I'll serve a fat slice of country pâté from my friend Russ Flint's Rain Shadow Meats on a wooden board, or offer up pork rillettes in their flip-top jar with a Paris flea market spoon.

No matter what, a French-inspired charcuterie plate should have a little something sharp on the side: There is a reason that it's standard practice to get a mustard pot and a handful of cornichons with charcuterie in Paris. But those aren't the only options: Feel free to add in pickled raisins, or a tangle of pickled caperberries or pale green *piparras* peppers (not French, but Basque, and I just love their tanginess with a touch of heat).

And in the spirit of the new Paris, I'd serve my charcuterie with a biodynamic wine from the Rhone, like Gramenon Sierra du Sud.

Casual elegance at Le Baratin in Belleville, Paris

frilled lettuces, walnut vinaigrette, and chervil

1 large head beautiful lettuce, like red oak or butter

½ cup (120 ml) red wine vinegar, plus more to taste

2½ cups (250 g) new-crop walnuts (see headnote)

1 teaspoon Dijon mustard

1 shallot, minced

¾ teaspoon salt, plus more to taste

Lots of freshly ground black pepper

1½ cups (360 ml) really good olive oil

1½ loosely packed cups (20 g) picked chervil leaves

Serves 4

Sometimes looks are everything. When it comes to lettuce, you want glossy, you want texture, you want a little variation in color. In France, even the most basic lettuces look pretty good, but you can afford to be choosy, especially if you go shopping at a great farmers' market. I seek out giant and beautiful frilled lettuce including butter and red oak. Another trick to salad greatness is to use tender herbs like they are another kind of lettuce. A favorite salad herb of mine is chervil, which has a little bit of anise flavor—like tarragon, but gentler. It's one of those herbs that's a cinch to grow—even in a pot—but hard to find in the grocery store, so think about scattering some seeds this spring. And a little note on nuts: Most walnuts tend to be old and often rancid. If you are lucky and can buy them from a farmer, they will have a sweet, almost brown sugar–like taste and much less bitterness. It's well worth it to shell them yourself. Otherwise get nuts from the bulk bin from a store that sells a lot of nuts.

Dismantle the lettuce head, discarding any bruised or damaged leaves. Immerse the healthy leaves in a very large quantity of cold water, swish, and let them sit for a few minutes. Lift the leaves from the water, drain the water, and repeat until no dirt gathers at the bottom of the water. Spin the lettuce dry and lay it on clean kitchen towels to dry. Store it in the refrigerator until ready to serve.

In a blender, buzz the vinegar, 1 cup (100 g) walnuts, the Dijon, shallot, salt, and pepper to make a coarse paste, then, with the motor running, slowly drizzle in the olive oil until blended.

In a large bowl, dress the greens with the vinaigrette, a little bit at a time, tossing gently with your hands and adding more vinaigrette as desired. Check the seasoning and add more salt and vinegar, if needed. Toss in some of the remaining walnuts, then transfer, if needed, to a serving bowl. Top with the remaining nuts and all the pretty chervil. Any extra vinaigrette can be stored in the refrigerator for 1 or 2 days.

leeks vinaigrette with capers and chervil

5 leeks, trimmed and halved
   lengthwise with core
   intact
½ cup (120 ml) olive oil, plus
   more to drizzle
¼ cup (60 ml) Champagne
   vinegar
1 tablespoon Dijon mustard
Salt and freshly ground black
   pepper
2 tablespoons capers,
   preferably salt-cured,
   rinsed, soaked for
   10 minutes, and drained
2 large hard-boiled eggs,
   grated (see page 21
   for my preferred method)
About 6 sprigs chervil
4 scallion tops, thinly sliced

Serves 4

There couldn't be a more classic Paris bistro dish, and no wonder: Leeks are sweet, cheap, hearty, and surprisingly quick to cook. They want a truly punchy dressing like this one. Then I like to have fun with the toppings—why not go overboard with green and layer in capers and chervil and a few scallion tops, too?

Bring a large pot of salted water to a boil. Place the leeks in the water and cook until bright green and tender but not mushy when poked with the tip of a paring knife, about 5 minutes. Remove the cooked leeks to a plate and let cool to room temperature. (It is OK to place them in the fridge if you want to hurry things up!)

Whisk together the olive oil, vinegar, mustard, salt, and pepper to make the vinaigrette.

Gently toss the leeks with all but a few spoonfuls of the dressing, lift them from the bowl, and arrange them on a serving platter. Spoon the remaining vinaigrette over and around the leeks.

Sprinkle the capers atop the leeks. Top the salad with the grated eggs, chervil, sliced scallions, more pepper, and a drizzle of olive oil.

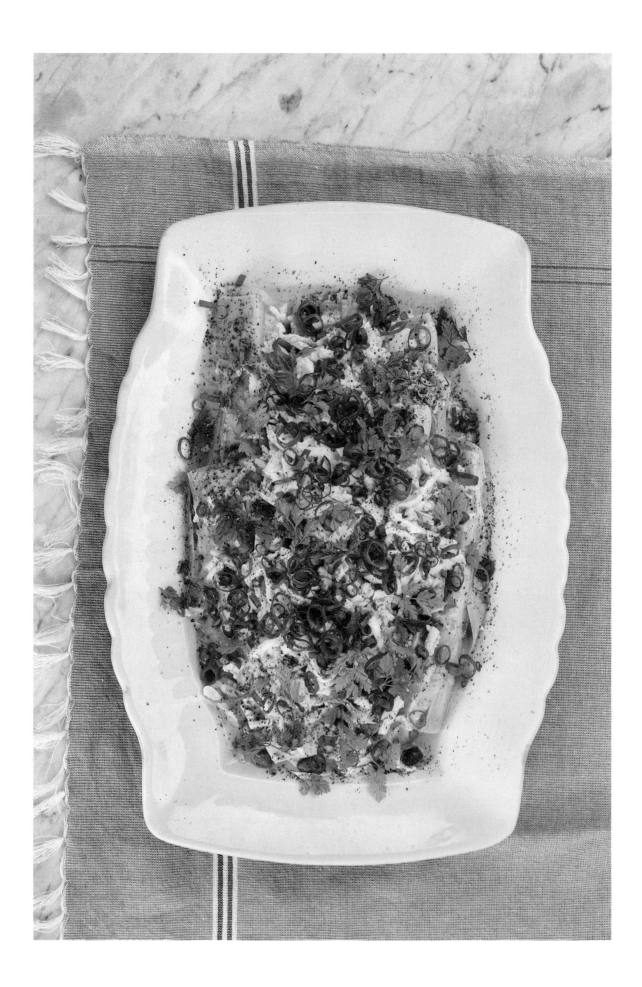

king oyster mushrooms with marjoram, bread crumbs, and poached egg

King oysters are a great mushroom to work with—succulent and moderately priced compared to wild finds like porcini. (By all means, make this with porcini if you have them. Make sure to invite me over, too!) A lot of natural wine bars in Paris have strong selections of aromatic whites, and this earthy dish would be a dream with them. Wines from the Alsace region should be pretty easy to find—I love Albert Boxler's wines, especially his Chasselas and crémant. You can also seek out more esoteric delights, like Julien Labet's Côtes du Jura Fleur de Savagnin or André & Michel Quenard's Chignin Blanc from the steep limestone slopes of the Savoie.

In a blender, buzz together the toasted bread, grated garlic, 1 tablespoon of the butter, and a pinch of salt to make fine but irregular crumbs.

In a heavy-bottomed skillet at least 10 inches (25 cm) wide over medium-high, heat the olive oil and 3 tablespoons butter. Once the butter starts to melt and sizzle, add the mushrooms and lightly season with salt. Cook, turning often so the mushrooms brown evenly, about 6 minutes. Add the sliced garlic, lemon zest, and preserved lemon. Sauté for another 2 minutes, then toss in the lemon juice. Warm through for 30 seconds, then turn off the heat.

Start poaching the eggs per page 341; while they are cooking, turn on the heat under the mushroom pan to medium high, bringing the mushrooms back up to a sizzle. Add all but a pinch of the marjoram and stir. Once the mushrooms are hot and the marjoram just wilts, spoon them into a serving bowl.

Place the poached eggs on top of the mushrooms. Season the eggs with salt and pepper.

Heat the remaining butter over medium-high heat in the mushroom pan; when it melts, add the remaining pinch of marjoram. When it sizzles, pour over the eggs and mushrooms. Finish the dish with a sprinkle of bread crumbs.

1 (1-inch/2.5-cm) slice rustic sourdough bread, toasted until dry and cracked into several pieces

2 garlic cloves, grated, plus 3 garlic cloves, thinly sliced

5 tablespoons (70 g) unsalted butter

Salt

2 tablespoons olive oil

½ pound (225 g) king oyster mushrooms, sliced in half

Zest from ½ lemon

Rind and zest from ¼ preserved lemon (available at villajerada.com), minced (save the scooped-out pulp of the lemon for another use, like braising meat)

1 tablespoon freshly squeezed lemon juice

2 Poached Eggs (page 341)

3 tablespoons fresh marjoram leaves

Freshly ground black pepper

Serves 2

smoked sockeye salmon with celery root and grainy dijon

1 grapefruit-size celery root, peeled and shaved into thin, wide ribbons

2 cups (480 ml) Grainy Dijon Vinaigrette (page 337)

Salt and freshly ground black pepper (optional)

1½ cups (340 g) Pickled Onions (page 341), drained

1 cup (20 g) Italian parsley leaves

1 (8- to 10-ounce/225- to 280-g) smoked wild sockeye salmon (my favorite is Lummi Island Wild Sockeye) broken into pieces; it will fall apart naturally with a little pressure

Serves 2 to 4

Sometimes it's a very small shift that makes a dish seem new. I've loved shredded celery root remoulade salads for years, but when I visited Le Café de la Nouvelle Mairie, a favorite modern, but not too modern, wine bar near the Pantheon, they served a lovely hunk of mackerel atop a salad of celery root cut into thick ribbons, not shreds. The sturdier shape gave the salad more presence alongside the rich fish, and it just looked great, too, with a few slices of pickled onion placed jauntily on top. Mackerel is a great fish but takes a little more effort to source than another favorite of mine, hot-smoked salmon. Of course, I'll only serve wild salmon, never farmed salmon, which is an ecological mess and full of medicine and dyes.

In a large bowl, toss the celery root with most of the dressing, reserving some of the vinaigrette to finish the salad. Taste and add salt or pepper, if desired.

On a serving platter, layer the celery root mixture with the pickled onions, parsley, and salmon, spooning on extra bits of vinaigrette as you go.

clams with dijon broth

½ cup (120 ml) Dijon mustard
2 cups (480 ml) white wine
2 tablespoons unsalted butter
2 shallots, thinly sliced
2 pounds (910 g) Manila clams, scrubbed
½ cup (240 g) crème fraîche
Fine sea salt and freshly ground black pepper
Freshly squeezed lemon juice (optional)
1 tablespoon fresh thyme leaves, to garnish

Serves 4

Mustard. Clams. Two things I love, but I hadn't tried together before. And so I was delighted with a bowl full of tiny cockles I had at Au Passage; the mustard rounds out in the clam juice to make a rich, slightly mysterious broth. Cockles are hard-shelled clams, about the size of a thumbprint. With pronounced ridges, they are very attractive but awfully hard to find on the American market, so I make my version with Manila clams instead. As with all brothy shellfish, be ready with bread to sop up the goodness.

In a measuring cup or small bowl, whisk together the mustard and white wine.

In a large pot with a lid, melt the butter over medium heat. Add the shallots and cook until tender and translucent, about 2 minutes. Pour in the mustard mixture and let cook for 3 to 4 minutes, until reduced by about one-quarter. Add the clams and cook, covered, for 3 minutes. Move any opened clams to a serving bowl, then cover the pot again for about 30 seconds. Move any opened clams to the serving bowl. Repeat until almost all the clams are opened; discard any clams that refuse to open after 5 minutes.

Reduce the temperature to low and whisk in the crème fraîche. Season the broth with salt and pepper (be cautious with the salt, since the clams may bring plenty of salt to the broth). Add a bit of lemon juice, if desired, to bump up the acidity. Increase the heat and bring the broth to a rolling boil, then pour the liquid over the clams. Garnish with fresh thyme leaves and serve right away.

halibut with anchovy butter

1 cup (2 sticks/225 g)
    unsalted butter, at room
    temperature
10 salt-packed anchovy fillets,
    rinsed and chopped into
    a paste
2 tablespoons capers,
    preferably salt-packed,
    rinsed, soaked for
    10 minutes, and drained
1 preserved lemon, pith and
    pulp removed, minced
1 pound (455 g) halibut
    fillet (in one large piece;
    ask your fishmonger to
    remove the skin for you)
Salt
3 or 4 sprigs marjoram,
    snipped into 1-inch
    (2.5-cm) pieces
½ cup (25 g) slivered garlic
    scapes, if in season, or one
    whole peeled garlic clove

Serves 4

The flavored butter here is hard to make in a small quantity, so you will have enough extra to stash in the freezer. People think a good bit about their pantry, all the canned and jarred and dried things that can make a meal out of nothing, but I hope they don't forget about their freezer, which can swoop in to save the day when last-minute meals come up. Take this dish, which is centered on an irresistible compound butter flavored with capers, anchovies, and preserved lemon. You could make it the day of cooking, but it's even more appealing just waiting there for you, ready to embellish a gorgeous hunk of fish that you discover at the market. You'd be ready to make delicious potatoes, root vegetables, or steak with this on hand, too.

In a stand mixer fitted with the paddle attachment, beat the butter on medium speed until fluffy and soft. Add the anchovies, capers, and preserved lemon. The butter can be made 3 days ahead and stored in the refrigerator or freezer until use.

Heat the oven to 450°F (230°C). In a large oven-safe non-reactive skillet, heat half of the anchovy butter over medium-high heat until slightly foamy. Add the halibut top side down and season lightly with salt. Cook undisturbed for 4 minutes.

Flip the halibut, season lightly on the browned side, add another tablespoon of the anchovy butter, and spoon the melted butter atop the fish. Place the marjoram and the garlic scapes in the pan in the butter.

Transfer the pan to the oven. Roast for 4 minutes, or until the fish is no longer translucent at its thickest point. This is delicious right out of the oven but also just as good at room temperature.

on top of paris
with dorie

No one enjoys time in Paris quite as completely as beloved cookbook author Dorie Greenspan. She and her husband, Michael, have kept an apartment in Paris for decades, and last summer, I had the chance to visit them at their current place in the 6th arrondissement.

To get to her flat, you have to take the world's tiniest elevator up, up, up to the top of a six-story apartment building, and when I walked in the door, she shoved a gougère onto my hand to "test." She was figuring out a new oven and trying to see if it was true to temperature. Her galley kitchen is tiny, so petite that the modest-size fridge is in the hallway. We stepped up and out the kitchen window to a tiny terrace with a tiny breakfast table and two tiny green chairs. Suddenly nothing was tiny anymore: Hers is the kind of Paris rooftop view that is usually only seen in movies about glamorous cat burglars. We shared a toast and savored the golden glow of the setting sun. As we climbed back into the kitchen, Dorie showed me her microwave, asking, "Isn't it great?" It took a moment to realize what she meant, but there, reflected in the dark glass of the microwave door, was the rooftop view—from the Pantheon to the Eiffel Tower and beyond.

That night we planned to go out to dinner, but first Dorie showed us how a proper *apéro* hour works—in addition to the gougères, she went to her favorite *charcutier* for some goose terrine, had picked up some exquisite cheeses at her *fromager*, and Michael had some chilled chardonnay ready to pour.

That could have been dinner, if we lingered longer, but Dorie is never done checking out intriguing spaces around the city. We headed to Le Grand Bain clear across the city in Belleville, a place I had just heard of, and of course Dorie had already been once before. With its wall full of windows, Le Grand Bain opens up to the street on a warm night.

Behind the glass wall to the kitchen, onto which is written the night's menu, we spied the British chef Edward Delling-Williams boogying behind the pass. The small plates of food were so bright and distinct: raw mullet in pretty ruffles mingled with lightly pickled cucumbers and roasted wild rice, cockles afloat in buttery broth with a pungent salsa verde, and fried baby shrimp coated in malt powder to eat shell and all, every bit as addictive as kettle corn.

When we talked to Delling-Williams, he was bursting with enthusiasm. Paris is awash with renegade urban gardeners that he is working with: There's the guy who's growing mushrooms in the basement of an old parking garage, a farm that's developing on the roof of a next-door building, and a team growing cresses and herbs in an old hospital. Everywhere in the city seems ripe for rebirth.

And Dorie, who seems younger each time I meet her, manages to savor longstanding traditions even as she samples everything that's new. I only hope to capture a sliver of her joyful curiosity.

norma

cider, super briny oysters, and cow's milk

Sometimes, while driving through Normandy, the road dips below the level of the hedgerow, and the trees reach their branches together high overhead to form a tunnel of dappled shadow. Even on a bright day, the effect is startling—ominous and beckoning all at once. This play of light and dark is echoed throughout the region. It's not uncommon for the sky to be bright blue on one side of a hilltop while dark clouds streak rain on the other. In a single morning, the sea can vary from almost tropical to foreboding, steely black-green. Even the architecture has this dark-and-light theme: Normandy is famous for its *colombage*, half-timbered construction, which alternates dark wood with patches of light plaster.

To me, Norman food also dwells in contrasts. There's the bracing side of it all: the sharp prickle of a briny oyster, a crisp cider, or the long, slow combustion of an aged Calvados. Then there are those big, cushioned, kind of autumnal flavors: caramelized apples, buckwheat, rosy grass-finished beef, and so much

good butter. Ingredients are extraordinary in Normandy—there are so many dedicated farmers, fishermen, and food artisans in the region—so I just look for easy ways to frame them beautifully.

Normandy has been a very important touchstone to me since I first planned to open the Walrus and the Carpenter. I came to delve deeper into the oyster traditions along the Atlantic coast, where the oysters are grown on raised beds in the open ocean. Pulled right out of the ocean, Norman oysters are much brinier than Pacific Northwest oysters, which are raised in estuaries and are softened in flavor by the fresh water running into the sea. Unlike in most parts of the United States, oysters aren't exotic in Normandy; they are just everywhere. In resort towns like Deauville and Trouville-sur-Mer, you can eat oysters at a fancy restaurant, but you can also dig in right at the open-air fish market, too. I love that sense of casual extravagance, and try to bring some of that spirit back to my businesses in Seattle. Thanks to the warmth of Norman friends like Stephane Le Bozec, an oyster salesman, and Thierry and Caroline Pic, event planners who run a beautiful vacation rental where I love to stay, I very soon felt at home there.

I am more likely to prepare my own meals when I'm traveling in Normandy. Unlike Paris or London, where I want to be out and about, Normandy is a place I go to hunker down. Maybe for one meal, I'll bathe in the amazing art deco–disco kitsch at Les Vapeurs, a seafood brasserie in Trouville. (While you're there, keep it simple and order the herring and the mussels; the fish market across the street is the place to go for oysters and *bulots*.) Mostly, though, I try to allow time for being still.

The last time I visited, I rented a two-hundred-year-old farmhouse, up a winding road and at the top of a hill above Pont-l'Évêque. Outside, wandering around below the apple trees, were a flock of stuttering sheep, plus a few clusters of chickens and ducks. Thyme, mint, peonies, and roses clustered around the patio, and inside, there were big, rough-hewn beams in the ceilings and not one, but two, hearths in the main living area.

One day when we had picked up an extraordinary steak on an outing, Jim, whose beautiful photographs illustrate this book, got to setting up a fire. We combed through the pile of CDs and put a Bach chorale on the boombox, and Jim found the grate from the grill outside. I seasoned the steak with nothing more than salt and pepper, and when the coals were mellow and ashed over, put it on the grate, with just a few coals below. I love cooking with live fire—there are so many sensations to take in: the scent of the smoke and tallow, the crackle of the mellow fire, the gentle scratch of the thyme bouquet I used to baste the steak with melted butter. With such a big steak, the pacing was easy—we had time to peek at the wind sweeping through the treetops in the darkening sky, to drink aperitifs, and to nibble on a few potato chips.

This was a vacation mode of cooking, but it's a way to rethink cooking for friends, too. Sometimes it's nice to have everything ready in advance, but sometimes, it's nice to slow down and cook something very special with ease and attention—the project itself gathers everyone together in conversation. And just a little bit of choral music can make the whole thing a bit more dramatic.

calvados sidecar

A simple way to let your Calvados shine. Pedestals, like in this photo, are optional but fun.

---

6 ounces (180 ml) Calvados
2 ounces (60 ml) Cointreau or
    other orange liqueur
1 ounce (30 ml) lemon juice
2 pretty lemon peels, to
    garnish

Makes 2 cocktails

Chill two coupe glasses in the freezer. Fill a cocktail shaker with ice and add the Calvados, Cointreau, and lemon juice. Shake very well until the shaker is almost too cold to hold. Strain into the very chilly coupes. Garnish each glass with a large strip of lemon peel.

Whale Wins Old Fashioned

calvados and tonic with lemon peel

Break away from gin and tonics and explore a new spectrum of super-refreshing cocktails. Calvados works so well with the bittersweet mixer—the bubbles help lift the apple-y aroma. For this drink, see if you can find a Calvados from Domfront, an inland region near the border with Brittany—it's an appellation that includes some pears in the Calvados and is particularly aromatic.

2 ounces (60 ml) Calvados
2 strips of lemon peel
4 ounces (120 ml) tonic water

Makes 1 cocktail

In a rocks glass filled with ice, stir in the Calvados, lemon peel, and top with tonic. Give one last stir and enjoy.

whale wins old fashioned

There was a time when I first started to visit Normandy with some frequency when there was a mismatch between the Calvados that I loved there and the slim selection of non-vintage options I had here. Then I found a little bit of Camut Calvados available from one of my distributors, and I snapped every bit of it up. I liked it so much I wanted to spotlight it at Whale Wins when it opened, and so we developed an Old Fashioned made with Calvados instead of whisky—with a kiss of sweetness and bitters to better accent the apple-y aromatics. Fortunately, the breadth of good-quality Calvados available in the United States (even online!) has increased greatly. Use the largest ice cube you can make for this drink. There are nice silicone molds for a giant cube available—I love to have them at home, not just at a fancy bar.

2 ounces (60 ml) Calvados
2 dashes angostura bitters
½ teaspoon Simple Syrup
   (page 21)
1 large orange

Makes 1 cocktail

In a rocks glass with a big ice cube, pour in the Calvados, bitters, and simple syrup. Stir it with a long spoon for about 30 seconds to dilute the drink just the right amount, and then peel a strip of orange while holding the orange over the glass, trying to aim the spraying oils into the glass. Place the peel in the glass to garnish.

honfleur

3 ounces (90 ml) Calvados
2 ounces (60 ml) elderflower
    liqueur (or you can
    use elderflower syrup,
    bumping up the Calvados
    to balance the sugar in the
    syrup)
6 ounces (180 ml) dry
    sparkling wine, like
    Crémant de Bourgogne
2 wide strips of lemon peel

Makes 2 cocktails

Honfleur is the name of a beautiful medieval port town on the Normandy coast. As you drive up from it into the hills of the Pays d'Auge, the hedgerows are often laced with big elderflower bushes, *sureau* in French, whose sunny fragrance merges with the grass and orchard blossoms. This drink tries to create a similar effect. You can make your own elderflower syrup by steeping fresh elder blossoms—if you are lucky to have some in your garden—in simple syrup, or purchase a cordial; Giffard makes a lovely one.

Fill a cocktail mixing glass about halfway with ice. Add the Calvados and the elderflower liqueur. When the glass is good and frosty, strain the liquid into two wineglasses, then pour in the crémant and the peel of lemon. Drink up while it's cold.

horse race

1½ ounces (45 ml) Simple
    Syrup (page 21)
4 mint sprigs, plus a bit more
    to garnish
4 ounces (120 ml) Calvados
1½ ounces (45 ml) lime juice
Club soda, to finish
2 lime wheels, to garnish

Makes 2 cocktails

Not far from the famous horse track in Deauville, my friends Thierry and Caroline have an exquisite house in the Norman countryside with climbing roses, neat yew hedges, a perfect green carpet of lawn, and my favorite: a lovely croissant-eating donkey named Chocolat. They introduced me to this bright cocktail, which gets a little zest from crushed mint and a squeeze of lime.

In a cocktail shaker, muddle the simple syrup with the mint sprigs. Add the Calvados, lime juice, and ice to fill. Shake vigorously and strain into two highball glasses. Add some ice and then top up with a splash of club soda. Garnish with the lime wheels and a few more sprigs of mint.

Honfleur

the apple-y beverages of normandy

Normandy is not customarily a winemaking region, but it has a long tradition of apple- (and pear-) based ciders, brandies, and cordials. Calvados is, of course, the star of the show.

On a hilltop just outside the harbor town Honfleur, there is the beautiful twenty-hectare (about fifty acres) orchard of Manoir d'Apreval, where Agathe Letellier produces wonderful ciders and Calvados. I visited her in the season when climbing roses were blooming on the half-timbered farmhouse, so I didn't get a chance to see the river of apples bob along a watercourse, and up into the sleek stainless cider press in the production room, but a few sips of her bright cider helped me imagine the process.

Agathe told us about the careful blending of bitter, bittersweet, sweet, and acidic apples to meet the standards of the Pays d'Auge region's cider production. Cider in that region must contain 70 percent bitter or bittersweet apples: "We can't make acidic cider in the Pays d'Auge," says Agathe, where the oxidation of the apples gives the iconic cider a round, honeyed quality.

As proof of the saying "what grows together goes together," rich ciders from the Pays d'Auge, many of which can be found Stateside (look for the DOC label), are glorious with complex cow's milk cheeses and fragrant steamed shellfish. (And for the record, since Manoir d'Apreval is not yet exported to the States, a couple of my other favorite Norman ciders are those from the producers Hérout and La Chouette.)

Some of the cider is sold as such—in pretty bottles with the Manoir's signature *colombage* as a logo. Other cider is distilled into higher alcohol spirits and barrel aged in the darker corners of the facility. There it becomes Calvados, the potent golden brandy. There's a tradition at a big Norman meal of the *trou normande*, the "Norman hole." That's a shot of Calvados swallowed to hollow out some room for the rest of the dinner.

We learned more about Calvados at La Cave Honfleuraise, where Marianne Denis walked us through several flights of the spirits, from the bright, searing-green apple bite of unaged Calvados to the mellower golden burn of five-year

Manoir d'Apreval, Pays d'Auge Normandy, France

the apple-y beverages
of normandy *(continued)*

Calvados, and the long-simmering caramel warmth of older-still Calvados. The bottle age of the Calvados tells consumers how old the youngest Calvados in a barrel is—a blend of twenty-, ten-, and five-year-old Calvados would still be called five-year-old Calvados. After each sip, Marianne encouraged us to toss any remaining drops in the glass onto the barrel where we were tasting, to perfume the store!

Calvados is made in three AOCs, and only in Normandy. I have spent the most time in the Pays d'Auge, where the Calvados is known for its fine honeyed tones that have been twice-distilled in alembic stills. I also really love the Calvados of the Domfrontais region, which gets roundness from the inclusion of more pears among the apples. Apparently, farmers in the region were so frequently augmenting their Calvados with pears, despite appellation rules, that in 1997, a new AOC was created just to accommodate the style.

I love to sip on aged Calvados on its own, but it's great in cocktails, too; I usually work it into drinks as if it were a whiskey, but it tends to be less weighty and woody than grain-based alcohols. I'm always eager to try a new Calvados, but I have some favorites, including the Camut 6-Year (or really any year), Lemorton 10-Year, Dupont, and Pierre Huet. For making the cocktails in this section, I would use a Calvados with a bit of age (five to six years), but not anything too ancient and precious.

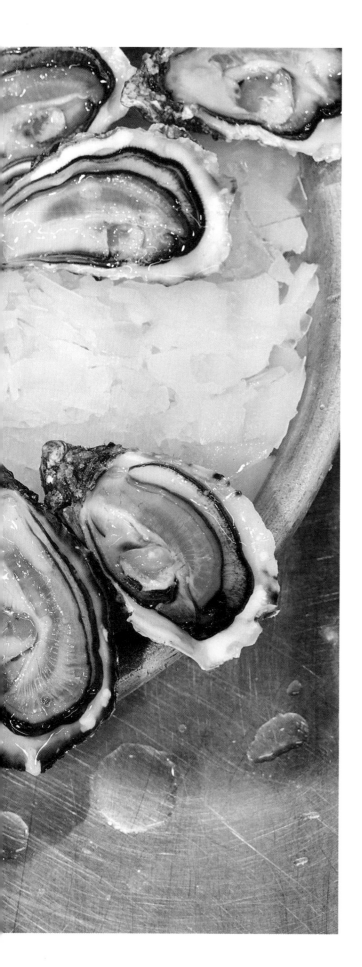

mignonette

1 large shallot, finely minced
1 cup (240 ml) Katz sparkling wine vinegar or a
    delicious Champagne vinegar
Lots of finely ground black pepper

Makes 1¼ cups (300 ml)

In a bowl, stir together the shallot, vinegar, and black pepper. Pop in the refrigerator and let the shallot macerate for at least 30 minutes before serving; serve within 1 day of making.

unlocking the oyster

To shuck an oyster American style, from the hinge, which is how we do at my restaurants (French oyster shuckers pull a trickier side-maneuver), first, make sure to clean your oysters in cold running water with a brush to remove any little clods of mud. Keep them with their scooped side down as much as possible.

To open, grab a clean kitchen towel folded in half, your oyster knife, gloves (especially if you're new to the technique), and a place for your clean oyster to land, like a tray covered in crushed ice or rock salt.

For a right hander, lay the towel across your left hand and place an oyster on it cupped side down and with the hinge facing toward your wrist. (The hinge is the tapered side of the oyster.)

Using your right hand, insert the tip of the knife into the hinge—there is usually a slightly depressed groove to guide the placement of the knife. Press into the hinge lightly until it sticks. If you're finding resistance, don't try to muscle through: Adjust your angle or the placement slightly and try again. Once it sticks, rotate the knife right to left to get it to pop open. You should not be pushing forward, but rotating side to side.

Once it pops open, wipe the knife blade with the towel, then use it to scrape along the right side of the top shell to cut the oyster's adductor muscle free. Remove the top shell, wipe the knife again, and trace along the right side of the bottom shell to cut the muscle there. Keep the shell as level as possible to prevent losing the juices. Keep an eye out for flecks of debris, and use the knife point to remove them before placing on the serving platter.

Left handers will need to start with the oyster in their right hand, and the directions will be otherwise reversed, too.

Don't wait to serve oysters—they should be eaten promptly after shucking.

chilled mussels with mint pistou

There's not much that's prettier than a mussel shell. In France, I've often seen mussels cooked, chilled, and placed back in their shells to make lovely hors d'oeuvres. It might be topped with a sharp mustard sauce or a bright green drop of mint pistou, which gives a springy contrast to the rich taste of the mussel while still amplifying the richness of the sweet meat.

The key to good mussels is editing them ruthlessly. Only use small blue-black Mediterranean-style mussels—not the big, old green ones. Just before cooking, rinse them well in cold water and inspect each one. Pull off any fibrous beards, squeeze each mussel to make sure it isn't damaged, and jostle it to make sure it clamps shut—if it doesn't pull shut with a little pressure, throw it out. Throw out any cracked-shell mussels, too. Once they are prepped, mussels couldn't be easier to cook.

2 garlic cloves, sliced, plus 2 garlic cloves, roughly chopped

2 cups (480 ml) dry white wine

2 pounds (910 g) mussels, scrubbed, debearded, and thoroughly checked for cracks

2 cups (80 g) basil, large stems removed, roughly chopped

½ cup (25 g) mint leaves, roughly chopped

1 cup (240 ml) olive oil

½ teaspoon salt

Crunchy sea salt, to finish

Serves 6 to 8

In a large, heavy saucepan with a lid, bring the sliced garlic, wine, and mussels to a boil over high heat. Reduce the heat to medium-high and cover. Steam the mussels for 3 to 4 minutes, until they have all opened. You can pull out the cooked ones into a separate bowl, and then cover the pot to allow the slow ones to cook a bit more. Toss out any mussels that don't open after 3 to 4 more minutes. Allow the mussels to cool in the cooking liquid. Once at room temperature, place in the refrigerator and chill for at least 1 hour, up to overnight.

In a blender, combine the basil, mint, olive oil, salt, and chopped garlic. Buzz together to create a smooth paste. Store the pistou in the refrigerator for up to 1 day until ready to use.

Carefully pull each mussel from its shell. Keep the beautiful shells to use as little serving bowls. Make sure to look in each mussel to pluck away any remaining beard if there is one.

In each shell, place a spoonful of the pistou, then the mussel and a drizzle of the green oil that floats atop the pistou. Sprinkle each mussel with a couple of grains of crunchy salt and serve right away.

bloomy-rind cheese with boozy prunes

8 to 10 ounces (225 to 280 g)
   prunes, the best you
   can find (chefshop.com
   carries lovely prunes from
   Southwest France)
1 cup (240 ml) Armagnac
1 wheel rich, bloomy-
   rind cheese, such as
   Kurtwood Farm Dinah's
   Cheese, Pont-l'Évêque,
   Camembert, or Fougerus,
   at room temperature
1 batch Moroccan Spiced
   Walnuts (optional;
   page 150)

Serves 6 to 8

We have a hard time sourcing good Camembert here in Seattle, and we certainly can't get raw-milk Camembert like that from Champ Secret. Import laws and, frankly, scarcity keep it in Europe for all but the lucky smuggler. But my friend Kurt Timmermeister keeps Jersey cows on Vashon Island, near Seattle, and he makes a luscious bloomy-rind cheese from their milk. Another reasonable option is to seek out imported Camembert from French cheese specialist Hervé Mons—it will be pasteurized like all soft cheeses sold in the States, but Mons is a famous *affineur* (cheese specialist) and it is better than many other imports. If you have managed to sneak a great Camembert into the country, then enjoy it this way, too. Another thing worth bringing back from France? Good prunes, particularly the semi-dried Prunes d'Ente du Lot-et-Garonne from Marc Peyrey—they are gorgeous, sweet-tart gems that are a stellar gift and much easier to bring home than contraband cheese! In this delicious presentation, they take a bath in Armagnac, the full-bodied brandy from Southwest France.

Place the prunes in a bowl and pour the Armagnac over them. Let the prunes macerate at least 2 hours (or overnight), turning gently every 30 minutes or so for the first couple of hours. The prunes can be refrigerated for a week before using.

Serve with the cheese and some spiced walnuts, if you desire.

moroccan spiced walnuts

8 ounces (225 g) shelled
walnuts
1½ tablespoons ras el hanout
¾ teaspoon salt
1½ tablespoons olive oil
1 tablespoon honey

Serves 4 to 6

Though most of Normandy's flavors are quite homegrown, it's not uncommon to find some far-flung spices in baked goods, condiments, or snacks, like these nuts. I suspect the seafaring ways of the Normans led to a rich palette of spices to work with. Back home in Seattle, I rely on my own globe-trotting friend, Mehdi Boujrada, to bring back incredible spices from Morocco, including fragrant *ras el hanout*, the blend of many, many spices, including saffron, rose petals, and cardamom. Tossing something this complex onto walnuts before toasting almost seems too easy, but it makes for such an addictive snack and dinner-party gift.

Heat the oven to 300°F (150°C). In a large bowl, combine the walnuts, ras el hanout, salt, olive oil, and honey and toss very well. Arrange the nuts on a baking sheet and toast, shaking the pan occasionally, about 15 minutes, or until they are slightly golden at their centers. Once cooled, the nuts can be stored in an airtight container at room temperature for a day or two.

quince compote

½ cup (120 ml) freshly
    squeezed lemon juice
4 large quince (3 to 3½ pounds/
    1.4 to 1.6 kg total)
4 cups (800 g) sugar
½ teaspoon salt
1 star anise

*Makes about three 1-pint
(500-ml) jars*

Quince is a bit of a mysterious fruit. You can't eat it out of hand—it's so tannic that it would take your breath away. But with time and cooking, it turns rosy and delicious. I love it with warm, fall-like spices as a counterpoint to a hunk of good cheese or a nice plain cake.

Have ready a large bowl of cold water mixed with 2 tablespoons of the lemon juice. Peel and core the quince, placing each in the lemon water as you go.

Cut the fruit into pieces about ½ by ¾ inch (12 mm by 2 cm), returning them to the lemon water until ready to cook. Drain and place the cut quince into a large, nonreactive saucepan and cover with fresh water. Bring to a rolling boil, then reduce the heat to simmer for about 15 minutes to soften. Drain the fruit, reserving 3 cups (720 ml) of the cooking water.

Pour the cooking water into a pot, and over medium heat, add the sugar and stir until dissolved. Add the salt, remaining lemon juice, star anise, and the quince. Simmer on low heat for 30 to 40 minutes, stirring often to make sure the bottom does not burn. The quince is ready when the syrup is thickened and the quince is glossy. Store the quince in its liquid in airtight containers in the refrigerator, up to about 1 month.

scallop cru with radishes and crispy shallots

2 cups (480 ml) canola oil or other neutral oil

4 shallots, peeled and thinly sliced crosswise

Salt

¾ pound (340 g) dry pack scallops (about 6 U-10 scallops), mostly defrosted, sliced into ¼-inch (6-mm) rounds

1 tablespoon plus 1 teaspoon extra-virgin olive oil

1 tablespoon plus ½ teaspoon freshly squeezed lemon juice

4 tablespoons (60 ml) crème fraîche

3 plump radishes, very thinly sliced

Crunchy sea salt, to finish

Serves 4

I can't leave scallops out of the Normandy shellfish conversation—the *coquilles St. Jacques* from the Calvados region, harvested only in the cold-weather months, are coveted throughout France. Back home, of course, we have some pretty great scallops to work with, too, and I love them sliced thin and raw, or *cru*. This dish is a pretty accumulation of circles, but the radish slices and the bittersweet scallion rings serve another purpose: Scallops can be easily overwhelmed, and so I thought up this dish, which added crispness and textural interest to the silky sweetness of the scallops without any aggressive flavors. Here's a tip for a lovely scallop slice: Cut them when they are still a little frozen (or if you have purchased them fresh, freeze them for an hour before cutting). Voilà, no raggedy edges.

Have ready a plate lined with a piece of paper towel. In a small saucepan over medium-low, heat the canola oil and the shallots. Cook at a gentle bubbly heat, stirring occasionally, until deeply golden brown, about 30 minutes. This is a long, gentle cook, not a quick fry—be patient! Using a slotted spoon or a spider, lift the shallots out of the oil and onto the paper towels. Season the shallots with salt.

Toss the scallop slices with 1 tablespoon of the olive oil and 1 tablespoon of the lemon juice and a pinch of salt.

Spread the crème fraîche across a serving platter. Lay the raw scallops across the crème in a single layer. Place the radish slices across the scallops. Drizzle the 1 teaspoon olive oil and ½ teaspoon lemon juice over the radishes and scallops. Sprinkle with a small bit of crunchy salt, and then top with the crispy shallots.

potted shrimp

This dish is where one part of Normandy I love (the sea) meets another (the extraordinary, extra-dense butter of Northwest France). Dairy is elemental in Norman eating, from cheese to butter to cream, and I love to watch spotted Normande cows grazing under apple trees, with a view of the English Channel whenever they bother to look up. In Europe on both sides of La Manche, there are small shrimp that can be eaten shell and all (or not!). In Britain they are called brown shrimp. In France, *crevettes gris*. Here, we don't have quite the same availability; but it's easy to find sweet shelled bay shrimp—often from Oregon or Maine. They are delightful in their own way, and of course, even more so when embedded in a little pot of butter, ready to be spread on rye bread.

1 cup (2 sticks/225 g) unsalted butter
1 bay leaf (fresh if you have it in your garden!)
1 long strip lemon peel
4 sprigs thyme
½ teaspoon salt
¼ teaspoon cayenne pepper
10 ounces (280 g) cooked bay shrimp
Freshly ground black pepper, to garnish
Warm rye bread, to serve

Serves 6 to 8

In a small saucepan over medium heat, melt the butter and let simmer for about 3 minutes, until the milk solids start to brown. Remove from the heat and let the butter settle for 5 minutes. Strain the butter through a fine-mesh strainer, letting the milk solids stay behind in the pan. They can then be discarded.

Pour the clarified butter into a clean saucepan, reserving ¼ cup (60 ml), and add the bay leaf, lemon peel, thyme, salt, and cayenne pepper. Let simmer over medium-low heat for 2 to 3 minutes.

Remove the pot from the heat, add the shrimp, and stir them with the butter. Remove the bay leaf and lemon peel and divide the shrimp among 4 ceramic ramekins or one larger dish. Put in the fridge to cool and firm up. When firm, pour the reserved clarified butter evenly over the shrimp and chill again. This will help preserve the shrimp, which can be stored, covered with plastic wrap in the refrigerator, up to 2 days before serving.

Take out of the fridge 1 hour before serving. Crack black pepper over the top of the potted shrimp and serve with warm bread.

Robert et Denis Andronikou Fish Market, Trouville-sur-Mer Normandy, France

plateau des fruits de mer

(Chilled Seafood Platter)

In Normandy, oysters are so much a way of life that there is a refrigerated oyster vending machine by the side of the main road into Trouville. Some of the machine's cubbies just stocked oysters, while others had lemons and knives for, I suppose, spur-of-the-moment picnics or other oyster emergencies. It's that complete appreciation for oysters that drew me to Normandy in the first place.

Last time I was there, I joined my friend Stephane Le Bozec for an oyster feast at Poissonnerie Robert et Denis at the seafood market in Trouville. It's a marvelous seafood stand with glistening fin fish, shellfish, and, naturally, a wide variety of oysters grown in the racing tides off Normandy's historic beaches, including Utah Beach, where Americans landed on D-Day. We sat at a table under the awning, a bottle of Chablis chilling, while Stephane, who sold oysters in Paris for years, teased open the shells and made an exquisite array for us. He stuck some Canadian- and American-flag toothpicks in the ice, too (the anniversary of D-Day had just passed). We also had small brown shrimp that we ate shell and all and chilled *bulots*—large sea snails—*à l'ancienne*, or long-cooked with a bit of cayenne, right there at the fish market. A big bowl of mayonnaise was there for the dipping. Sitting on the sidewalk with Stephane, Robert, and his son Alexandre, savoring the extra-briny Normandy oysters at ten on a chilly Normandy morning was an unforgettable breakfast!

At the fish market, our astonishingly good seafood was served on paper plates, but elsewhere in Trouville, and at many of the restaurants in the beach towns of Normandy, they offer tremendous chilled seafood platters, stacked not just with raw oysters and clams, but shrimp, langoustine, lobsters, spider crabs, and so, so many bulots.

It's so fun to take inspiration and make your own *plateau de fruits de mer*. If you have a tiered platter, go for it, or use your biggest serving tray. Cover it with crushed ice, and if you have some seaweed handy drape that over the ice. Then lay down a combination of raw and cooked seafood. Use whatever chilled seafood tastes great and is in season in your part of the world. I'll always have oysters, but depending on what's fresh, I could add raw clams (hard to open but delicious), poached shrimp, steamed spot prawns or langoustines, slow-cooked bulots, steamed periwinkles if you can find them, cooked crab in quarters, or cooked lobster. The many specialized implements that French restaurants offer to help you pick your seafood are elegant, but forks, fingers, and crab pincers are usually the only tools I want.

Then, all you need is a bowl of mignonette (page 143) for the raw seafood, a bowl of mayonnaise or aioli (see Lemon Aioli, page 338) for the cooked bits, and lots of lemon wedges. And, as always, keep some good bread and butter nearby.

Even in the apple capital of Normandy, wine is traditional with chilled shellfish: usually Loire whites or a really crisp Chablis like the one we enjoyed in Trouville. Open some Champagne, though, if you are feeling festive.

mussels with vadouvan curry

2 tablespoons unsalted butter

4 shallots, sliced into thin rounds

¼ cup (25 g) Vadouvan curry powder

2½ cups (590 ml) white wine

½ teaspoon salt

3 pounds (1.3 kg) mussels, scrubbed, debearded, and thoroughly checked for cracks (see headnote, page 147)

Baguette, to serve

Serves 4 to 6

Vadouvan is a masala spice blend with a French accent—lots of shallot—that most likely evolved from the French colonial presence in the region around Pondicherry. It has familiar curry flavors like fenugreek, cumin, and mustard, but a notable roundness, too, that adds depth and aroma to a simple pot of steamed mussels. The resulting ochre broth looks beautiful against the blue-black mussel shells. Make sure to serve with a crackly baguette.

In a large saucepan or braising pan with a lid over medium heat, melt the butter. Add the shallots. Stir well and sauté for 2 minutes. Stir in the Vadouvan and toast for 1 minute, stirring often. Whisk in the wine and salt, bring to a simmer, and cook for 1 minute.

Add the mussels, cover the pot, and steam for 3 to 4 minutes, until they have all opened. If necessary, pull the open ones out and cook for another minute or two to allow the laggards to open. Discard any mussels that do not open after 4 minutes.

Dish the mussels and the broth into serving bowls and serve right away with the baguette.

coal-roasted beets with salt-rubbed cabbage

1 pound (455 g/about ½ head) cabbage, cored

2 tablespoons plus 1 teaspoon kosher salt, plus more to taste

6 to 8 medium beets, skin on, scrubbed

1 (6-inch/15-cm) horseradish root, peeled

5 ounces (140 g) crème fraîche

7 tablespoons (105 ml) olive oil, plus a little extra to garnish

Freshly ground black pepper

3 tablespoons sherry vinegar

½ cup (50 g) Italian parsley leaves

1 piece long pepper (optional; available at worldspice .com)

Crunchy sea salt, to garnish

Serves 4 to 6

I just love cooking over coals. It's the last, lazy phase of live-fire cooking. Whole ingredients need just an occasional turn, and then back to conversation and cocktails for a while. In the coals, they get chewy and caramelized on their exteriors, while their interiors steam and tenderize. Toss them with salt-rubbed cabbage and some lush horseradish cream, and you've made an uncommonly satisfying meat-free dish to serve friends who want to hang out by the firepit with you.

Separate the cabbage leaves and sprinkle with 2 tablespoons of the salt. Massage the salt into the leaves. Let rest for an hour, occasionally massaging the salt into the leaves. After an hour, rinse the salt from the cabbage and dry in a salad spinner or by placing in a tea towel and swinging it around.

Build a charcoal fire in the grill and let the coals burn until they are all gray. Nestle the beets among the coals and cook for 20 to 30 minutes, using tongs to turn them occasionally, until the beets have softened but remain a little firm at the center when poked with a paring knife. Remove to a heat-proof platter and let cool to room temperature.

Grate about 1 cup (80 g) of the horseradish, reserving the rest for garnish. In a small bowl, combine the grated horse-radish with the crème fraîche and 1 teaspoon of the salt.

Slice the cabbage leaves into fat ribbons about 1 inch (2.5 cm) thick. In a large bowl, toss the cabbage with 3 table-spoons of the olive oil and black pepper. Peel the beets and cut into quarters. In another large bowl, toss the beets with the remaining olive oil and the vinegar. Season with salt and black pepper.

Arrange the cabbage on a large platter, then pull the beets out of their marinade and arrange in and around the cabbage. Dollop the horseradish cream on the vegetables. Top every-thing with the parsley leaves. Spoon some of the beet mari-nade around the edge of the platter and drizzle the top of the salad with a little additional olive oil. Grate some additional horseradish on top, as well as long pepper, if using. Finish with a sprinkle of crunchy salt.

savory buckwheat flour crepes with leeks, apples, and pont-l'évêque cheese

1 batch Crepes (page 336)

4 tablespoons (55 g) unsalted butter

3 large shallots, sliced into 6 wedges each

Salt

2 medium baking apples, cut into ¾-inch (2-cm) wedges

8 ounces (225 g) Pont-l'Évêque or other soft, bloomy-rind cheese, trimmed and pulled into small pieces

1 tablespoon fresh thyme leaves

Crunchy sea salt, to finish

Serves 4

Brittany, next to Normandy, is known for its crepes made from *blé noir* ("black flour"), or *sarrasin* ("buckwheat"). Buckwheat has an intense, moody flavor that makes for a great foil to rich flavors. In both regions, buckwheat crepes, called galettes, serve as a base for savory fillings like cheese, eggs, or ham. We serve a lot of them at Bar Melusine. The crepes can be made ahead and refrigerated for a day or two (feel free to freeze them for up to a couple of weeks; they thaw overnight in the refrigerator).

Make the crepes according to the instructions.

Melt 2 tablespoons butter in a pan over medium heat. Season the shallots with a bit of salt and cook slowly, turning them every so often. They are ready when they have a little color but are not very brown, about 5 minutes. Wipe out the pan and melt 2 more tablespoons butter over medium heat. Place the apples in a single layer and cook slowly, flipping once, until the wedges are browned on both sides, being careful not to cook so much that the apples burst, about 8 minutes total.

Heat the oven to 500°F (260°C). Have ready a baking sheet lined with parchment paper. Working with one crepe at a time, put about a quarter of the cheese in the middle, making a 3-inch (7.5-cm) square of cheese. Top with 2 to 3 slices each of shallot and apple, and sprinkle with some fresh thyme.

Fold in the round edges of the crepe to make a square, using the edge of the cheese as a guide for where to crease. Press gently to make the edge lie down. Place on the sheet pan folded side down and repeat with the remaining crepes. Top the crepes with any remaining bits of cheese and drizzle a bit of extra butter from cooking the apples. Cook for 5 minutes. Garnish with a bit of crunchy salt before serving. Eat while hot!

Plenty of space and a varied meadow for the Normande cattle at La Ferme du Champ Secret, one of France's most treasured Camembert producers

asparagus with sauce gribiche

2 pounds (910 g) asparagus

3 tablespoons capers, preferably salt-packed, rinsed, soaked for at least 10 minutes, then drained and chopped

2 tablespoons Dijon mustard

3 tablespoons white wine vinegar

¼ cup (60 ml) olive oil, plus extra to garnish

20 cornichons, chopped

Salt and freshly ground black pepper

1 cup (240 ml) Lemon Aioli (page 338)

4 large hard-boiled eggs (see page 21 for my recommended method), coarsely chopped

¼ cup (13 g) chopped Italian parsley leaves, plus more to garnish

¼ cup (13 g) chopped tarragon, plus more to garnish

¼ cup (10 g) chervil leaves, plus more to garnish

Juice of ½ lemon, to finish

Lemon wedges, to serve (optional)

Serves 4 to 6

The hilly countryside of Normandy's Pays d'Auge has so many layers of green, it's astounding. Clover green, grass green, oak leaf green, apple leaf green, hydrangea green—you get the idea. This dish isn't explicitly Norman, but it does also have many layers of green, from the asparagus to the capers to the chervil. *Sauce gribiche* is one of my favorite French sauces, because it has so many appealing little tidbits: luscious eggs, salty capers, tart cornichons, and, of course, an extravagance of herbs. It's great on so many things—from fish to root vegetables to cold beef.

Bend the asparagus near the bottom of each stalk: They will snap where the tough base ends. Trim each end flat. Have ready a medium bowl filled with ice water. Set a steamer basket into a large, lidded saucepan. Add water, stopping ½ inch (12 mm) below the steamer basket. Bring water to a boil and lay the asparagus in the steam pan; cover tightly and cook until the asparagus is crisp but tender, about 2 to 5 minutes, depending on the thickness of the spears. Remove the thinner spears first and then the fatter spears, checking doneness with a pointy knife—the asparagus should be tender but still a bit firm. Place the cooked asparagus in the ice water to cool rapidly. Once cool, drain and pat the asparagus dry and store in the refrigerator until ready to serve, up to 1 day.

In a large bowl, whisk together the capers, mustard, vinegar, olive oil, cornichons, salt, and pepper. When ready to serve, fold in the aioli, chopped eggs, parsley, tarragon, and chervil. Taste and add a little lemon juice and a bit more salt or pepper, if needed. Place the asparagus on a serving platter. Spoon the sauce on top, allowing the tips and tails of the asparagus to peek out. Garnish with extra olive oil and herbs and serve with lemon wedges, if desired.

sardines, shaved lemon, and walnut salad

2 (4.2-ounce/120-g) cans oil-packed sardines, drained well

1 cup (250 g) shaved fennel bulb, tossed with a squirt of lemon juice to keep it pale and bright; reserve the fronds to garnish

1 organic lemon, half shaved thin on a mandolin, seeds removed, keep the other half to squeeze

10 pickled piparra peppers, sliced into little rounds

¼ cup (60 ml) olive oil

Salt

¾ cup (75 g) toasted walnuts

Buttered grilled bread (optional)

Serves 2 to 4

You might be getting the picture by now: I highly recommend having sardines available for inspired, spur-of-the-moment eating. Marking them in a hot grill pan before serving them crackles the skin and warms up the flavors nicely.

Heat a grill pan over the highest heat. Place the sardines across the ridges and grill until marked on the bottom, about 2 minutes. Very carefully turn the sardines over and mark again, about 2 more minutes. Place on a serving plate.

In a large bowl, combine the fennel bulb, lemon slices, and piparras. Toss with the olive oil, a squeeze of lemon juice, and a big pinch of salt. Taste and adjust the seasoning with more salt or lemon juice if desired.

Lightly pile the salad on the sardines, pulling up a bit to keep the salad from smooshing down. Scatter with walnuts and fennel fronds to finish. Of course, if you want to put the whole thing on buttered grilled bread, that's fine, too!

endive gratin with air-cured ham

Endive is such a relief in the winter, when the produce is so dominated by the sweetness of root vegetables and winter squash. Raw endive is fresh and juicy with just the right amount of bitterness. It's also such a lovely winter white. When it is cooked, its flavor intensifies into both sweet and savory directions. To make this baked dish even more luscious, I bundle each endive wedge in a thin wrap of fancy ham.

In a medium saucepan over medium heat, warm the cream with the nutmeg, cayenne, and salt. Keep a careful eye: If the flame is too hot, it will boil over. Simmer for about 40 minutes, or until reduced by half.

Heat the oven to 350°F (175°C).

In a large skillet over medium-high heat, melt the butter, and place the endives cut side down. Cook until the cut edges are toasty brown. Place the endives, cut side up, in a baking dish that will hold them snugly. Squeeze each endive half with the lemon and bake for 10 minutes, or until cooked through.

Remove from the oven and let cool. When you can handle them, remove the endives one by one and wrap with a slice of ham, placing each back in the baking dish.

Drizzle the wrapped endives with the reduced cream. Grate the Parmigiano generously over the top. Return to the oven and bake for another 30 minutes, until bubbly and brown.

This can be served right away, but is also delicious when cooled, refrigerated, and reheated the next day.

2 cups (480 ml) cream
¼ whole nutmeg, freshly
    grated
Pinch of cayenne pepper
Salt
4 tablespoons (55 g) unsalted
    butter
6 heads Belgian endive,
    halved lengthwise
½ lemon, to squeeze
4 ounces (55 g) sliced
    air-cured ham, like
    La Quercia or prosciutto
1 cup (25 g) rasp-grated
    Parmigiano-Reggiano
    cheese

Serves 6 to 8

slow-braised shallots with cider

3 pounds (1.4 kg) shallots
4 tablespoons (55 g) unsalted
    butter
1 tablespoon olive oil
1 tablespoon Dijon mustard
2 cups plus 1 tablespoon
    (500 ml) dry apple cider
6 thyme sprigs
Salt and freshly ground black
    pepper

Serves 4 to 6

Cider tastes so good with Normandy's iconic foods—shellfish, rich cow's milk cheeses, and beef—but it's also a fantastic ingredient to cook with. Something as simple as shallots are transformed with cider, thyme, and time, too, to become pink, jewel-like, and translucent. These are great as a side dish, but they can also be pulled apart into petals to serve as a scoop for smoked fish or pureed with chicken stock for a fancy little soup.

Heat the oven to 350°F (175°C).

Peel all the shallots, keeping them as whole as possible.

In a large sauté pan over medium heat, melt the butter with the olive oil. Place the shallots in the pan and slowly sauté, turning and stirring fairly often, until gently browned, about 8 minutes.

Transfer the shallots and all the buttery pan juices into an ovenproof baking dish (about 8 by 12 inches/20 by 30.5 cm).

In a small bowl, whisk the mustard into about 1 cup (240 ml) of the cider. Add this mixture and the remaining cider to the dish. Add the thyme and season with salt and pepper. Braise, uncovered, in the oven until tender when pierced with a knife, about 50 minutes. Serve warm, or store in the refrigerator for a couple days. Warm before serving.

fireplace-cooked steak
with thyme butter

2½ pounds (1.2 kg) bone-in rib-eye steak

½ cup (1 stick/115 g) unsalted butter

A bunch of thyme, tied with twine

Salt and freshly cracked black pepper

Crunchy sea salt, to serve

Serves 2 as an entrée, or 4 as one of several plates

Near my friend Stephane's house in Dives-sur-Mer is the shop of butcher Vincent Ouzouf, who patiently showed us around his shop one day. He is a rare butcher-farmer, who raises his own grass-finished Blonde d'Aquitaine and Limousin cattle. He told us he grew up caring for sheep at his family's farm and he wanted to become a farmer, but as he got older, he understood that it would take more than farming to make a living in today's world. Being a butcher gave him the means to start farming.

Of course, I had to try one of his steaks, so I picked out a huge *côte du boeuf* and brought it back to the farmhouse in the hills five miles (8 km) away. I cooked it over the coals in the fireplace, tending to it over the gentle fire for a good long while, and letting it rest for almost as much time before carving it. Cooking in the fireplace is a magical experience, and it's worth the effort from time to time. You can't get a steak quite like Ouzouf's here, but try a grass-finished bone-in rib-eye cut, and you won't be disappointed. If you can find a steak as burly as the one in the picture, which weighed about 4 pounds (1.8 kg), you will need more time to cook it, but it won't be quite double the time of the 2½-pound (1.2-kg) steak I call for here. Just keep turning it every 6 to 8 minutes to keep the cooking slow and even. You can find a campfire grill online, or you could use your barbecue grate set onto bricks to make this work.

Start your fire and pull the steak out of the refrigerator about 30 to 45 minutes before you want to start cooking. Build up the fire to make a solid bed of coals. Push the burning logs to one side and pull the red and gray coals over to where you want to cook your steak. Place a grill about 6 inches (15 cm) over the coals and let it heat up for about 5 minutes before you set down the steak. Place the butter and the thyme bundle (you will use it like a brush) in a little saucepan in a warm spot near the fire, where the butter will soften.

Season the steak generously with salt and freshly cracked pepper. Place the steak on the grate and grill on one side for about 6 minutes. Flip the steak—make sure at this point that it is browning gradually, not scorching. If it is cooking

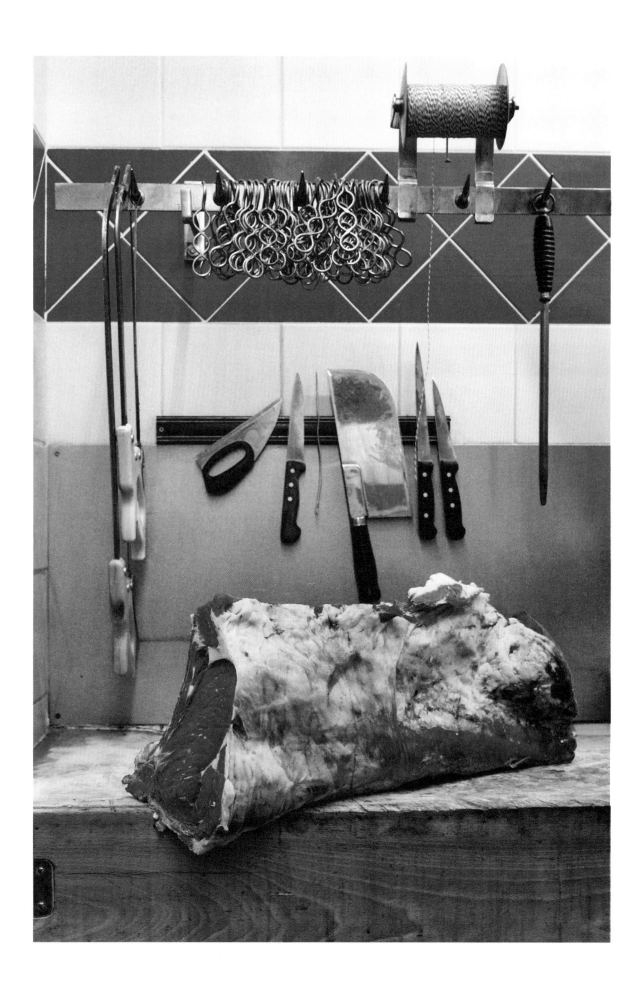

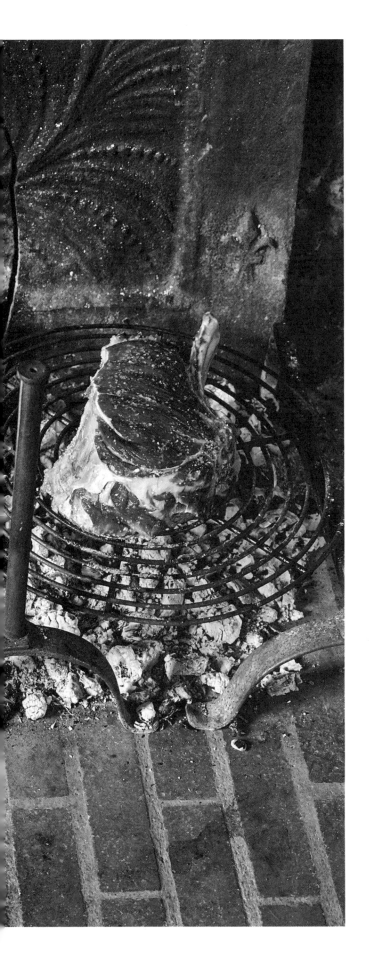

fireplace-cooked steak with thyme butter *(continued)*

too fast, move some coals to make the heat less intense. Use the thyme bundle to baste the steak with butter. Cook on this side for another 6 minutes, and then flip again. Baste with butter each time you flip. Cook for 2 minutes, and then turn again. If your steak has a super thick fatty side, turn the steak up on this side to cook for about 1 minute, and then do the same on the bone side. In total, the cooking time should be no more than 15 to 16 minutes for medium-rare, less time for rare. For a medium-rare steak, pull it when a meat thermometer reads 120°F (49°C); the temperature will rise while the steak rests.

Remove to a cutting board and baste one more time with the butter. Cover the steak with a tent of aluminum foil to rest for about 20 minutes. Slice the steak off the bone and across the grain into chunky slices. Arrange on a warm serving plate, and drizzle, if desired with a little more thyme butter. Sprinkle with crunchy salt and serve.

boat street normandy chicken with buttered boiled potatoes

3 tablespoons olive oil

1 (4- to 4½-pound/1.8- to 2-kg) chicken, cut into 6 or 8 pieces

2 tablespoons kosher salt

Freshly ground black pepper

4 medium shallots, peeled

2 cups (480 ml) dry cider, preferably French

10 thyme sprigs

1 bay leaf

1 tablespoon Dijon mustard

1 large apple, cut into ½-inch (12-mm) wedges

½ cup (120 ml) cream

1 batch Buttered Boiled Potatoes (page 336), to serve

Serves 4 to 6

I created this dish long before I ever went to Normandy. It sprang into being after dreaming with cookbooks in my lap and the totems of Normandy in my mind: apples, cream, butter. Susan Kaplan, the original owner of Boat Street Café, had a similar dish made with prunes, but once I put the apple-y version on the menu, it never came off. People just adored the luscious sauce. It feels like I served millions of guests this dish; it's so decadent and rich. When I said goodbye to Boat Street in 2015, I also said goodbye to serving it on my menus. Here it is for you to make at home and serve to millions of your friends and family.

In a high-sided skillet over medium-high, heat the olive oil. Place the chicken pieces skin side down in the oil and season with the salt and pepper. Cook, turning and seasoning once during the process, until golden brown, about 10 minutes. Remove the chicken from the pan and set aside.

Add the shallots to the pan and cook until they gather a bit of color, about 2 minutes. Pour in the cider and scrape up any browned bits from the bottom of the pan. Add the chicken pieces back to the pan, along with any juices.

Reduce the heat to a simmer, add the thyme and bay leaf, and cover the pan. Cook for 15 minutes. Remove the cover and continue cooking until the chicken is cooked through, about 5 to 10 minutes. Remove the chicken to a plate and tent with aluminum foil.

Whisk the mustard into the broth, stirring thoroughly to make sure it doesn't curdle. Add the apple and simmer, uncovered, approximately 10 minutes. Remove the apple from the pan to the same plate with the chicken. Stir the cream into the sauce, increase the heat to medium-high and cook for about 5 minutes, until the sauce is thick enough to coat a spoon.

Return the chicken and apples to the pan and stir to coat over low heat to warm through. Serve on a big platter with the potatoes on the side.

the secret meadow

We panted a little as we climbed a high hill in the southwestern region of Normandy—clover and grass mingled in the meadow and the puffy clouds clustered ominously. Across the hillside strolled lovely cows, their coats mottled ivory, caramel, and darkest brown, and most with eyes strikingly ringed with dark fur. The ladies were quiet but for their sturdy munching. They weren't skittish at all, but, as Patrick Mercier pointed out, they were picky. His herd had enough room that they could avoid grazing near any cow patty or distasteful weed.

Mercier must struggle for excellence in the era of an industrialized cheese industry and thus the declining reputation of the region's—maybe France's—most famous cheeses. By crafting Camembert by hand, with unpasteurized milk, in pristine conditions, he is seeking to re-elevate the cheese.

Mercier is the owner and cheesemaker of La Ferme du Champ Secret, one of the last two raw-milk, farmstead Camembert makers in Normandy, and it is on that hilltop that his well-tended Normande graze on a special blend of clover and grass to make one of the most coveted cheeses in France. "This Camembert is very difficult to make, but it is very easy to sell," he says. The microflora that change from batch to batch mean each cheese has a slightly different personality from the last. "There are nothing but good surprises," says Mercier.

After visiting his meadows and production facilities, we finally get to taste the cheese produced in his field. We cut into one of his perfect rounds near the meadow and drank a cider alongside—one of those perfectly resonant food-and-beverage pairings. I could almost imagine the scent of apples in the cheese and a creaminess in the cider. Even if we can't source Mercier's or other raw Camembert in the States, I look to farmstead cheesemakers who share his dedication to animals and to flavor, like my friend Kurt Timmermeister of Kurtwood Farms on Vashon Island and other cheesemakers from other parts of the country, such as Shelburne Farms in Vermont, Uplands Cheese in Wisconsin, and Nettle Meadow in New York.

Norman cuisine is full of butter and cream and cheese, and it's easy to understand why, with its extraordinary landscape of meadows, orchards, and hedgerows. Mercier's farm is an exceptional one, but everywhere I travel in Normandy, I am greeted by uncrowded, glossy-pelted cattle.

At my Seattle steak restaurant, Bateau, we make sure the heritage-breed cattle farmers we work with raise cows with room to grow and thrive. At home, you can find more transparency by shopping your local farmers' market. Looking at the Norman countryside, I'm reminded that we aren't alone in trying to find a more humane and sustainable way to raise beef. France has industrial-scale agriculture, too, of course, but I'm inspired by these farmers who push back against the demands for speed and profit to produce meaningfully delicious food.

londo

garden herbs, gin, and clothbound cheddar

London is a whirlwind. I visit to see art-work, to see theater, to see markets, and to look for fixtures in the vintage home stores tucked around the sprawling city. Few places pulse with such a strong intensity. And maybe because of this, when it comes to eating and drinking, I am particularly drawn to spaces that create a sense of serenity. Whether it is a garden setting or just a fine-tuned dining room, the most luscious British places have a way of cultivating intimacy, calm, fun, and, of course, delicious food. The past several

Hidden courtyard at Rochelle Canteen, London

decades have seen British chefs digging into the culinary traditions that were endangered in the scarcity of the postwar years: heritage breeds of livestock, handcrafted preserves, and a distinct pride in the freshest seasonal produce.

Spring, for example, Skye Gyngell's restaurant at Somerset House, is one of my favorite restaurants in the world, with high ceilings, tall arched windows looking out into the busy city, and a spacious server station clad in striking book-matched marble (one of the most elegant I've ever seen!). The room could feel too splendid to relax in, but the servers, in Breton striped T-shirts, are somehow jaunty and professional at once. And the food, it's so good: gorgeous farm ingredients presented simply but poetically, garnished with leafy tendrils, fronds, and flower petals.

Bar Termini, not much bigger than a fancy closet, is tucked amid the noise and brashness of Soho, but inside, precise bartenders pour batched negronis into tiny, brimming glasses. The white jackets and the exacting bar-craft could feel a little fussy, but there's an easiness, too: Maybe it's the bouncing mid-century Euro-pop, or the smile of the host as he finds a small corner for us to wait for a seat at the bar.

And then there is Rochelle Canteen in Shoreditch, tucked in the former bicycle shed of an old school behind a garden gate.

No one knows how to make a guest feel at ease like Margot Henderson, the co-owner with Melanie Arnold, and one of my all-time entertaining role models.

The last time I went there, I had the luck to sit down with Margot at a weathered wood table under a grape arbor. A little-bit-unruly container garden grew near the tables, with variegated horseradish and fennel and geranium and foxgloves popping out of the pots. We ordered a late lunch, and Margot ended up chatting with us for the whole afternoon, making sure we had sun hats and that our glasses were never empty of delicious white Languedoc wine.

I love the way Rochelle Canteen serves big, sharable plates with just a few elements on them: fat asparagus with a big scoop of herby *gribiche* sauce, thin slices of pork topped with a tangle of mustardy celeriac ribbons, or poached sea trout served cold and flaky with big chunks of lightly dressed cucumber and fennel ribbons—all on plain white plates. There's such confidence and verve in this kind of boldly simple food. It makes you feel at ease digging in, grabbing an asparagus with your fingers, or scooping some salad out for your neighbors.

Every time I serve guests, I hope to combine familiarity with a little bit of marvel and make them feel just as welcome as Margot does.

cucumber-basil gimlet

4 (1-inch/2.5-cm) chunks of cucumber
6 basil leaves
4 ounces (120 ml) Plymouth gin
1½ ounces (45 ml) freshly squeezed lime juice
½ ounce (15 ml) Simple Syrup (page 21)
Pinch of salt
Cucumber flowers, to garnish, if available

Makes 2 cocktails

If you really want to emphasize the chilly side of a cocktail, it's hard to beat a cucumber—so here's my take on a classic gimlet. If you are lucky to have a cucumber vine in your garden, grab a couple of flowers for a sunny garnish.

Chill two stemmed cocktail glasses by filling them with ice.

In the bottom of a cocktail shaker, muddle the cucumber and basil. Fill the shaker with ice, then add the gin, lime juice, simple syrup, and salt. Shake well. Pour out the ice in the glasses and strain the mixture into them. Garnish each glass with a cucumber flower, if available.

dirty vermouth martini

8 to 10 green olives (I like picholines)
5 ounces (150 ml) London Dry-style gin
1 ounce (30 ml) olive juice
1½ ounces (45 ml) dry vermouth

Makes 2 cocktails

A big chair and a small, icy cocktail: That's luxury, and one reason I keep coming back to the bar at the Zetter Townhouse Clerkenwell. I really like their tiny, cold, cold, cold martinis with a generous share of vermouth in the gin. My version here has some olive juice tipped in and several olives—try picholines.

Fill two stemmed cocktail glasses with ice while you prepare the cocktails.

Load as many olives as can fit onto two cocktail picks. In a cocktail shaker filled with ice, combine the gin, olive juice, and dry vermouth. Stir for a while, say a minute, until the spirits are frigid.

Pour the ice out of the cocktail glasses, strain the martinis into the glasses, and garnish with the olives.

Dirty Vermouth Martini

gin fizz

½ ounce (15 ml) honey
 or Simple Syrup
 (page 21)
½ ounce (15 ml) lightly
 whisked egg white
¾ ounce (22 ml) lemon juice
1¾ ounces (52 ml) Plymouth
 gin
Soda water, to top

Make 1 cocktail at a time

If there's one thing I love, it's meringue. So, when I had my first gin fizz in New Orleans—with all that egg-white fluff floating on top—it really made my night. The only problem is that a gin fizz can give you a sore elbow from all the shaking it takes to get fluffy. Our bartender, Tommy Stearns, at Deep Dive gave me a new idea: Use a cheap little milk foamer device to pre-fluff the egg whites before shaking with the ice. Brilliant! You can still make a fizz without it, but your arm will get tired.

Chill a Collins glass by filling it with ice.

In a cocktail shaker, combine the honey, egg white, lemon juice, and gin. Use a little coffee foamer to mix and fluff the combination for 20 to 30 seconds, until very fluffed and foamy. Alternatively, place a lid on the shaker and shake for a full minute.

Scoop ice into the shaker and close it securely. Shake for 15 to 20 seconds, until the shaker is almost unbearably icy to hold.

Pour out the ice in the glass, and strain the fizz through a fine strainer into it. Let the fizz settle into the glass for 15 to 20 seconds, and then top the glass with soda water—letting the egg white rise as high as you dare.

White Port with Lime

lemon gin and tonic

I love limes, but unless I am in the tropics, they feel very specifically summer, so I craft my gin and tonics around lemons. And when I say lemons, I really mean it: I double the peel in this drink and give it a solid squeeze of lemon juice, too. Look for a London Dry–style gin—here in Seattle, I like our local Kur.

2 wide strips lemon peel
1½ ounces (45 ml) London
    Dry–style gin
3 ounces (90 ml) tonic
    (I like Fever-Tree)
Wedge of lemon, to squeeze

Makes 1 cocktail

In a rocks glass, place one strip of lemon peel. Fill the glass with your best ice. Place the second lemon peel atop the ice, then pour in the gin, followed by the tonic. Finish with a solid squeeze of lemon juice.

white port with lime

You can find delicious, honey-toned aged white ports to sip and contemplate, but you probably don't want to make an apéro with them. Look instead for unaged—and cheaper—white port that mixes well with tonic or, like here, dry vermouth. You can adjust the ratio to find just the right sweetness level for yourself.

3 ounces (90 ml) dry
    vermouth
3 ounces (90 ml) white port
½ ounce (15 ml) lime juice
2 slices lime, to garnish

Makes 2 cocktails

In a cocktail shaker filled with ice, stir together the vermouth, port, and lime juice. Strain into two highball glasses that are two-thirds full of ice. Garnish with the lime slices.

gin and all its personalities

On the whole, I like my restaurants serene and airy, but a good bar, especially a hotel bar, can be a little over the top. If the lighting is warm and low, I like overstuffed seating, rich colors, heraldry, and maybe some whimsical taxidermy. The Zetter Townhouse Clerkenwell has all that and a stuffed cat in a fancy blue dress. It's a great place to drink gin cocktails, too. The gin drinks are accented with potions that sound like they were brewed by woodland fairies, like nettle cordial and dandelion and burdock bitters. When I put together my own fancy-drinks bar, Deep Dive, I had in mind luxe and eccentric places like the Zetter: Blue velvet booths, curio cabinets curated by my friend, artist Curtis Steiner, and beautiful glassware all help make each cocktail feel like a slightly fantastic journey more than a drink.

Of course, gin is a key part of my image of Britain (even if the original gin, or *genever*, was a Dutch tradition). It's been a dominant spirit in the British drinking world since the late seventeenth century, when William of Orange taxed French imports like wine and cognac at a heavy rate. Other laws gave spirit-producers in England a tax break, so distilling became a very appealing business, and gin seeped into the culture. As the British Empire expanded, sailors and other colonial workers took Indian tonic water along with them to help ward off malaria. They combined it with their ration of gin, and made the combination a classic (throw in a lime to ward of scurvy, and it was all the better).

Gin is interesting to taste because of that tradition of aromatics, unusual for a clear spirit. It can be minimalist or, these days, infused with a national park's worth of flavorings. I favor a clean, bright London Dry–style gin with juniper and citrus as the primary flavors. More exotic ingredients—Douglas fir, seaweed, coriander—all have a place as long as things don't get too flowery—no need for prominent lavender in my gimlet, thank you very much.

There are more and more interesting gins from around the world, but British gins are hard to beat. London-made Sipsmith is dry with great baked citrus and coriander notes—it is my go-to London Dry-style. The Botanist, from Scotland, is balanced with woodland botanicals like sweet cicely and wood sage; Plymouth Gin is its own classic style—a gorgeous, slightly less bone-dry spirit with a bit of earthy spiciness.

With good gin should come good tonic. Grocery store tonic water is too sweet and chemically for my taste. Homemade tonic water is erratic and often distracting in a drink. I like to split the difference and stock up on good British tonic water. Fever-Tree Indian tonics are so good. Fentimans is harder to find but also delicious.

Finally, I prefer my gin drinks to be on the smaller size, like the perfect little negronis served at Bar Termini. Why? First, I am a bit of a cocktail lightweight; if I drink too big of a cocktail, I'll have to forgo wine at dinner, and I don't want to do that. Second, I am of the firm belief that coldness is the key ingredient in a gin drink. If my drink is too big, then it will warm up or dilute itself too quickly. And finally, there are all those pretty little cocktail glasses I pick up in vintage stores. Why wouldn't I want to use them?

I'll often order fortified wine—or a cocktail made from it—in London, too. Sherry apparently became popular in London because it was one of the things Sir Francis Drake seized from the Spanish fleet in 1587, while port took on more prominence in the 1700s—the same era as gin—when French wine imports were heavily taxed. For me, these fortified wines take me back to my early days at Boat Street, when they added a lot of complexity to a drink without a lot of work for the bartender (often me). You can spend a lifetime exploring port and sherry, and I encourage you to do so. In this chapter, I have a recipe for a refreshing port and vermouth, but you can try it with a modestly priced *amontillado* sherry, too—both are delicious!

Finally, I can't talk about drinking with London on my mind without mentioning beer. I am very much a wine drinker, but things like sharp English Cheddars and savory pies really do crave a brown malty ale. Skip the overwhelmingly hopped ales that are popular here in the States and try a not-too-cold Lord Marples bitter ale from Thornbridge Brewery or a classic can of Helles Lager from Harbour Brewing Co.

The Zetter Townhouse

giant cheddar gougères

1½ cups (360 ml) milk
½ cup (1 stick/115 g) unsalted butter
Pinch of salt
1¼ cups (155 g) all-purpose flour
4 large eggs
3 cups (345 g) grated sharp white Cheddar cheese

Makes about 6 gougères

These are really, really big gougères, which are slightly over the top in the most festive way. Gougères are French, of course, but these airy cheese puff pastries start to seem pretty British if you load them with great handfuls of very sharp Cheddar. If you can get your hands on some Neal's Yard Montgomery's Cheddar, lucky you! But if you can't, seek out an aged white Cheddar and bake away. They're good with a dirty martini or a glass of Champagne.

Heat the oven to 450°F (230°C).

In a small saucepan over medium-high heat, bring the milk, butter, and salt just to a boil. Add the flour all at once and stir vigorously to incorporate. Reduce the heat to medium and cook, stirring continuously, for 1 to 2 minutes, until the dough feels smooth and not too sticky, like Play-Doh when quickly pinched. Place the dough in a large mixing bowl and let cool for 5 minutes.

Using a wooden spoon, beat the eggs into the dough one at a time, making sure to incorporate the egg completely before mixing in the next. Stir in 1 cup (115 g) of the cheese.

Line a baking sheet with parchment paper or a silicone mat. Scoop the dough in 1-cup (240-ml) scoops onto the sheet, making sure to leave plenty of space around each—no more than 6 to a half-sheet baking tray. You can pause here and freeze the gougères on the tray until solid and then place in a zip-top bag until ready to bake. They will take a little more time to bake than if made from fresh.

Generously cover each gougère with a portion of the remaining cheese. It's OK if it falls to the parchment; it will crisp up and be delicious. Bake for 15 to 20 minutes, until the dough has puffed extravagantly. Rotate the tray and turn the oven down to 300°F (150°C), and bake another 15 minutes. Rotate the pan again and continue to bake another 10 to 20 minutes, until they are dark golden brown. You might want to go a little longer than you'd expect—developing a nice caramel color. Once cooked, use a cake tester or toothpick to poke 3 or 4 holes in each gougère so that it can release its steam without collapsing. Let them cool for at least 10 minutes before serving.

stilton with wheat crackers and marmalade

1 cup (125 g) whole-wheat
  flour, plus more for rolling
  out the dough
¼ cup (30 g) wheat germ
1 teaspoon baking powder
½ teaspoon salt
2 tablespoons brown sugar
½ cup (1 stick/115 g) cold
  unsalted butter, cubed
⅓ cup (75 ml) whole milk
1 pound (455 g) Stilton,
  removed from the fridge
  at least 1 hour before
  serving
½ cup (160 g) bitter orange
  marmalade, to serve
Freshly ground black pepper

Serves 4 to 6

Whole-wheat crackers like this, sold as digestive biscuits in the UK, are thick and sweeter than regular crackers—halfway to being a cookie. As a kid, I always picked them out of the Carr's cracker assortment my mother would set out at parties. When baked fresh, their toasty flavor is even more inviting and makes them a great partner for the sharpness and acidity of Stilton. Stilton is one of the great prides of British cheese-making, and because of its exceptional creaminess, has a gentle side that can coax even newcomers to the blue side of the cheese plate. Stilton stands tall in big wheels before it is cut, and a big hunk of it is so much better than the little precut selections you'll often find in the grocery store, smooshed up against their plastic wrap. Buy a big wedge—the texture will be nicer, and it's really exciting to look at the marbled cross-section of the cheese. If you have some crumbles left, you can make blue cheese dressing!

Heat the oven to 350°F (175°C).

In a food processor, combine the flour, wheat germ, baking powder, salt, and brown sugar and buzz for 15 seconds to combine. Add the butter and pulse until it forms a crumbly texture, about 20 seconds. Pour in the milk and process just until the mixture comes together.

Generously flour a work surface and place the dough on it, patting it into a nice ball as you do. You can wrap and refrigerate the dough at this point for up to a day before proceeding; pull it out of the refrigerator 30 minutes before rolling. Flour a rolling pin and roll the dough to about ⅛ inch (3 mm) thickness. Cut into 2-inch (5-cm) rounds using a cookie cutter or the top of a glass.

Place the rounds on a parchment paper–lined baking sheet. Prick the surface of each round with a fork a couple of times. Bake for 15 minutes. Remove to a wire cooling rack and let cool completely before serving. Store in an airtight container at room temperature for up to 2 days.

To serve, place the Stilton, marmalade, and a nice collection of the crackers on a serving platter. Top with a little pepper.

seedy brown bread and seaweed butter

2 cups (250 g) stone-ground
    whole-wheat flour
1½ cups (190 g) all-purpose
    flour
2 teaspoons salt
1¾ cups (420 ml) lukewarm
    water
1 tablespoon dark molasses
2½ teaspoons active dry yeast
½ cup (70 g) sunflower seeds
2 tablespoons poppy seeds
Canola oil, to grease the pan
Seaweed Butter, to serve
    (page 342)

Serves 4 to 6

Seaweed is everywhere in London these days, including a dish of smoked eel tucked beneath a translucent blanket of red dulse that I had at Lyle's, a chic restaurant that serves great British farmstead or seaside ingredients with restrained modern elegance. If you don't have fresh dulse on hand (and who does, really?), this compound butter is a simple way to bring some bright-but-rich seaweed flavor to your kitchen. It's great with bread and can also be melted into any number of cooked dishes.

In a medium bowl, combine the flours with the salt. Pour ⅔ cup (160 ml) of the water into a small bowl and stir in the molasses and yeast. Let stand until it starts to foam on top, about 10 minutes. Pour the yeast mixture and the remaining water into the flour mixture and stir until a batter is formed; it will have the consistency of cooked oatmeal. Stir in the sunflower and poppy seeds. Let it stand for 10 minutes.

Brush an 8½ by 4½-inch (20 by 11-cm) loaf pan with oil and cut a piece of parchment paper to line the pan, covering the two long sides and extending an inch (2.5 cm) or so above the edge on each side. Scrape the dough into the prepared pan, smooth the top with your dampened hand, and drape a kitchen towel over the top. Let it rise in a warm place until the dough reaches the top of the pan, about 20 to 30 minutes.

Heat the oven to 450°F (230°C).

When the dough has reached the top of the pan, bake the bread for 20 minutes. Reduce the heat to 400°F (205°C). Pull the pan from the oven, run a knife around the outside of the bread to release it from the pan, tip the loaf out of the pan, remove the parchment paper, and place the loaf upside down directly on the baking rack and bake another 15 minutes, or until done (when you tap the bottom, it should sound hollow).

Let the bread cool, if you can, before cutting into it. It's not easy to wait—but worth it, as it will help keep the bread moist over time. Serve the bread with the seaweed butter.

Store wrapped in plastic at room temperature for 3 or 4 days. It's great toasted for breakfast, too.

soft-boiled eggs, sage aioli, and fried sage

I always have too much sage in the garden. Sage, though Mediterranean in origin, is one of the most commonly used herbs in Britain—Elizabeth David called it, rather dismissively, "that very English herb." She didn't like it much, but I do. This earthy herb doesn't go with everything, but it's great with pork and poultry, and crunchy fried sage leaves are one of my favorite things in the world. Just to double up on the flavor, I make some mayonnaise with sage oil, too. A note on eggs: Fresh eggs are incredibly delicious, but they will drive you nuts if you try to peel them after boiling; this recipe will work best with eggs that have been out in the world for a few days.

3 large egg yolks, plus 8 large eggs
2 tablespoons freshly squeezed lemon juice
1 batch Sage Oil (page 342)
Fine sea salt
½ cup (120 ml) grapeseed oil
16 to 20 sage leaves
Crunchy sea salt, to finish
Olive oil, to garnish

Serves 6 to 8

In a quart (liter) container or a preserving jar, blend the egg yolks and lemon juice with an immersion blender. Slowly drizzle in the sage oil, pulling the hand blender up and down slowly through the jar to emulsify. Season with sea salt and, if desired, use a tablespoon or two of water to thin the aioli.

Have ready a medium bowl filled with ice water. Bring a medium pot of water to a boil and lower the eggs one by one gently into the water. Set a timer for 6 minutes once the water comes back to a boil. Remove the eggs directly to the ice bath. Once cool, peel, dipping each egg into the water occasionally to rinse away any shell fragments, and set aside.

Have ready a slotted spoon or a spider and a baking sheet lined with a wire cooling rack or a double layer of paper towels. Pour the grapeseed oil into a heavy-bottomed skillet and heat to 325°F (160°C). Place 8 to 10 sage leaves into the hot oil and cook until crisp, about 30 seconds. Remove them to the prepared sheet and repeat with the remaining sage leaves. Season the leaves with sea salt.

To assemble: Slice the hard-boiled eggs in half lengthwise. Place a dab of aioli on a platter beneath each egg half to keep them from sliding around. Season each egg half with crunchy salt and spoon a bit of aioli on each. Top each egg with a crispy fried sage leaf and a drizzle of olive oil.

prunes with goat cheese and bacon

6 ounces (170 g) fresh chèvre

24 prunes, pitted (good imported prunes are available at chefshop .com)

12 slices thick-cut uncured bacon, halved crosswise

Serves 8 to 10

Walking into Leila's Shop, located off Arnold Circus in Shoreditch, feels like a trip through time. Even the hazy sunbeams cutting past the cheese counter seem to be out of the past. I'm sure there's a computer in there somewhere, but if so, it's well camouflaged. The store is stocked lightly to contemporary eyes, and each artisanal product has an aura of specialness: the Sicilian lemons with their leaves still on in a crate outside the door, the few majestic cheeses on the counter, the stern but fetching country jams, the shatteringly crisp Spanish potato chips with great packaging. And then there are the prunes, kept in what looks like a pink jewelry box. Each one sparkles under the cellophane—dark, glistening, and about twice as large as your standard shriveled model. You have to ask the grocer to pluck each one out of the pink box for you and place it in your waxed paper bag to take home. Like any old-fashioned thing, they take a little more work to eat—the pits are still intact—but they are so succulent and tangy! Unless you live in London, it may be hard to get such carefully tended prunes, but no matter what, these snacks are irresistible, with the bacon and the creamy-tart chèvre setting off the rich dried plums.

Heat the oven to 350°F (175°C).

Pinch a bit of the chèvre and place it into the cavity of one of the prunes. Wrap the prune in a half-slice of bacon and pin with a toothpick. Repeat with the remaining prunes. Place the prunes on a baking sheet and cook 20 to 25 minutes, or until the bacon has crisped and the cheese is warm at the center.

toasty cheese and chile jam sandwiches

¼ cup (60 ml) mayonnaise

¼ cup (55 g) softened
  unsalted butter

4 thick slices good sourdough
  bread

⅓ pound (150 g) sharp
  Cheddar cheese, coarsely
  grated

4 tablespoons (60 ml) Fresno
  chile jam or other hot
  pepper jelly

Makes 2 sandwiches

You don't have to do much to delight your guests—olives and chips go a long way—but if you want to step up from room-temperature snacks, ooey-gooey cheese toasties (grilled cheese to us Americans) is a great start. They are so simple and so generous. For a crowd, just lay them on a cutting board and cut into strips for everyone to dig in. In this version, chile jam adds sweet tanginess and heat. I also learned a tip from my co-writer Sara's daughter, Adele, who at twelve is a prolific griller of cheese: Mayonnaise on the outside of the sandwich makes it easier to get a perfect crust.

In a small bowl, combine the mayonnaise and butter.

Heat a heavy iron skillet over high heat for 1 minute.

Take two slices of bread and spread one side of each with the mayonnaise mixture. Place the slices, mayo side down, into the skillet and reduce the heat to medium. Distribute the cheese evenly between the two bread slices.

Making sure to align the bread slices, cover one side of the remaining two slices with the chile jam. Lay jam side down on the cheese. Spread the top of the slices with the remaining mayonnaise mixture.

Cook until the bottoms of the sandwiches are nicely toasted, about 4 minutes, and then carefully flip. Cover the pan, reduce the heat to low, and continue to cook until the bread is toasted and the cheese is melted, about 4 to 6 minutes. Cut into halves or slender pieces for sharing and serve right away.

shrimp on toast with capers, dill, and chervil

There's something lovely and a little ridiculous about having a giant, open-faced shrimp sandwich, casual as chicken salad, like the one I had at Rochelle Canteen in the spring of 2019. It was piled high with the small brown shrimp that are very popular in London, tossed in a creamy dressing riddled with herbs. Sourcing the same brown shrimp is difficult in the States, so you either must go big—standard cocktail size—or get some tiny bay shrimp (I get mine from Oregon). They are a little sweeter than their British counterparts but also delectable. Seek out wild shrimp: They will taste so, so much better and are almost always a sustainable choice.

If using raw shrimp, poach them gently: In a medium saucepan, bring 3 cups (720 ml) salted water to a boil. Have ready a baking sheet lined with parchment paper. Drop the shrimp into the pan, reduce the heat to a very gentle simmer, and let cook for 2 to 5 minutes, until opaque almost all the way through. Remove the shrimp to the prepared baking sheet to cool. When cool, shell the shrimp and devein, and if using large ones, cut in half lengthwise. If using cooked shrimp, start here.

In a small bowl, combine the capers, crème fraîche, sour cream, salt, pepper, lemon zest, and most of the dill and chervil, reserving a bit to garnish. Toss the shrimp with the dressing.

Pile the shrimp high on each slice of bread. Garnish with crunchy salt, freshly ground black pepper, and some pretty picked herbs.

1½ pounds (680 g) shrimp, raw, shell-on, or cooked Oregon or bay shrimp

¼ cup (30 g) chopped capers (preferably salted, rinsed, soaked for 10 minutes, and drained)

¾ cup (180 ml) crème fraîche

¾ cup (180 ml) sour cream

½ teaspoon salt

¼ teaspoon freshly ground black pepper, plus more to garnish

Zest of 1 lemon

1 cup (50 g) dill fronds, lightly chopped, plus a few fronds to garnish

1 cup (40 g) chervil, large stems removed, plus a few fronds to garnish

4 (½-inch/13-mm) slices rye or sourdough bread or Seedy Brown Bread (page 202), grilled, cooled (see page 20 for some tips on toasting)

Crunchy sea salt, to finish

Serves 4

london market life

One of the great pleasures of staying in London, particularly the East End, is visiting the vibrant markets that pop up on certain days. They have more of a festival atmosphere than many markets in the United States, which is surely annoying if you are trying to get an efficient weekly shop in but can be quite fun if you switch to tourist-dawdling mode. Just steps from the canal in Hackney is the Broadway market on Saturdays. Past the racks of beachwear and tie-dyes, you can grab six fresh-shucked oysters from the Irish sea before sampling and purchasing cheeses, jams, pickles, hams, produce, and hipster peanut butter from vendors along the street. Food vendors sell Gujarati onion fritters, Scotch eggs, and Persian street food. The permanent shops along the market street are exciting, too: By day, Hill & Szrok is a butcher shop focusing on small-herd, whole-animal meat, but at night, the marble counters are cleared and dinner is served, using the parts that are typically harder to retail (think rump instead of ribeye). Next door, cooks seated behind the window of the Turkish café Saray roll yard-long *gözleme* flatbreads and then fill them and toast them with cheese and spinach to order.

You have to submit to the crowd at the Columbia Road Flower Market nearby on Sundays, but it is delightful to see the whole street transformed into a temporary garden of plant vendors singing jingles to sell their acres of hydrangeas and foxgloves. It's also hilarious to watch customers try to waddle home on foot with an oversize rubber-tree plant in their arms. Off the side streets, you can breathe a bit more and drink a Pimm's cup from a walk-up window as a street busker plays love songs on a clanky piano.

Maltby Street Market at the Ropewalk near London Bridge hosts a huge range of street-food stalls next to a railway bridge, and more permanent businesses charm customers from under the archways of the trestle. LASSCO is a huge, incredible architectural salvage shop, with vintage tile, lighting fixtures, and hardwood, which makes me start dreaming of a new restaurant interior. There's an alehouse, a natural wine bar, a Spanish *jamon bodega*, and multiple gin-tasting opportunities.

Borough Market is a wonderful old Victorian arcade, with well-established stops on the British food pilgrimage, like Monmouth coffee, the astounding Neal's Yard Dairy, and Kappacasein, famous for its toasties (more cheese, grilled this time!). There's a new food hall there, too, filled with delicious-sounding stalls that I can't wait to check out. But I'd recommend going on Wednesday or Thursday to avoid prime-time crowds.

Some of my favorite restaurants also run beautiful mini groceries, filled with nothing but lovely and tempting things. Honey & Co., the landmark Middle Eastern restaurant, sells produce, spice blends, grains, jams, wines, pastry, and fantastic takeout food at Honey & Spice. Quality Chop House, whose steaks and potatoes confit are beyond compare, has Quality Food, Wine & Butcher next door. From the chiller, you can get their legendary potatoes confit, all cooked and ready to brown in the oven; the butcher offers extraordinary chops and charcuterie; and the shelves heave with pantry staples, exotic condiments, and tinned seafood. A small selection of gorgeous produce and some well-chosen natural wines can round out your meal. At night, the wine shop becomes a perfect wine bar, with small delicious plates and the most genial atmosphere.

deep-fried green beans with calabrian chile aioli

1½ cups (350 ml) mayonnaise (I like Best Foods/ Hellmann's) or homemade Lemon Aioli (page 338)

3 tablespoons Calabrian chile paste

Salt

1 cup (125 g) all-purpose flour

1 cup (130 g) cornstarch

Freshly ground black pepper

1½ cups (360 ml) sparkling water, plus more if needed

About 8 cups (2 L) neutral oil like grapeseed, canola, or sunflower, to fry

1 pound (455 g) Romano beans or green beans

Lemon wedge, to serve

Serves 4

Maltby Street Market is a favorite stop of mine. Beneath garlands of flags, food stalls sell portable food of all sorts, from baps to falafel to briny British oysters. Underneath the arches of the bridge are more fixed businesses that allow visitors to step away from the merry madness of the market to enjoy some quieter moments. 40 Maltby Street is a wine bar in one of those long, cool archways, boasting a chalkboard menu of natural wines and masses of fresh-cut flowers—creamy pink peonies when I last visited. One of their dishes was a plate of fresh young fava beans fried in an airy batter. They were so crisp outside but vibrantly green and perky inside. What a great contrast! Fava beans tender enough to eat whole are pretty much a gardeners-only scenario in the United States, so I made my own riff with Romano beans—you could use ordinary green beans, too.

In a small bowl, whisk together the mayonnaise and the chile paste. Taste and add salt. Chill until ready to serve.

In a large bowl, whisk together the flour, cornstarch, and salt and pepper. Quickly whisk in the sparkling water. Place the mixture over an ice bath or in the refrigerator until ready to fry.

Have ready a pair of tongs and a wire cooling rack set over a baking sheet, or line the pan with paper towels, which you will need to change often. In a heavy 4-quart (4-L) saucepan or Dutch oven, heat 2 to 2½ inches (5 to 6 cm) oil to 370°F (190°C).

You will need to fry in batches: Place a handful of beans into the prepared batter and stir to coat. Working with one bean at a time, pick the beans out of the batter and lower into the hot oil. Increase the heat to high for 30 seconds to get the temperature back to 370°F (190°C), then reduce the heat to maintain the temperature. Cook the beans until the batter has crisped and the beans are crisp-tender, about 2 minutes and 45 seconds. Remove the beans to the prepared baking sheet and salt right away. Repeat with the remaining beans. Serve the beans while they are warm with the prepared chile aioli and a lemon wedge.

roasted shallots with mint leaves and grainy mustard

1 pound (455 g) plump
    shallots, unpeeled
½ cup (120 ml) plus
    1 tablespoon olive oil, plus
    more to garnish
½ teaspoon salt, plus more to
    taste
Crunchy sea salt
4 ounces (115 g) fresh goat
    cheese
2 tablespoons heavy cream
2 teaspoons grainy mustard
1 tablespoon white wine
    vinegar
Freshly ground black pepper
1 packed cup (50 g) mint
    leaves
4 (½-inch-/1.25-cm-) thick
    slices sourdough bread,
    toasted (see page 20
    for some tips on toasting)

Serves 4 to 6

I'd never had mint as a salad before I tried a dish very like this one at St. John, Fergus Henderson's classic, modern/traditionalist restaurant near the Smithfield market (he's married to Margot of Rochelle Canteen). It's such a clever use of a very common ingredient, which grows like crazy in my garden. The shallots, too, are unexpectedly lovely: roasted and then separated into pale pink petals. Guests assemble this salad bit by bit—a little bit of audience participation to make everyone feel more relaxed.

Heat the oven to 400°F (200°C).

On a baking sheet, coat the shallots with 2 teaspoons olive oil, and sprinkle with the salt. Roast for 35 minutes, until tender but not mushy. Let cool, then peel off the papery exterior. Halve each shallot lengthwise and toss with crunchy salt and 1 teaspoon olive oil.

In a stand mixer fixed with the paddle attachment, whip the goat cheese and the cream for 1 minute, until the mixture is smooth and creamy.

In a small bowl, whisk together the mustard and vinegar. Slowly pour in the remaining ½ cup (120 ml) olive oil while whisking to emulsify the vinaigrette. Taste and adjust the seasoning with salt and pepper.

In a medium bowl, dress the mint leaves with the mustard vinaigrette.

Spread the goat cheese mixture on a large platter. Top with the shallots and sprinkle with a few more flakes of crunchy salt. Drizzle with additional olive oil. Arrange the mint leaf salad to the side of the shallots. Bring to the table with the grilled bread and have your guests assemble their own toasts with a little bit of everything.

brandade and grilled bread

½ pound (225 g) Homemade
Salt Cod (page 338),
rinsed well

1 bay leaf

3 fresh thyme sprigs

2 lemons, halved, plus more
to taste

1 pound (455 g) Yukon Gold
potatoes, peeled, cut into
2-inch (5-cm) chunks
(keep in fresh water until
ready to cook to prevent
browning)

Salt and freshly ground black
pepper

¾ cup (180 ml) olive oil

2 garlic cloves, smashed

¾ cup (180 ml) warm whole
milk

Grilled bread (see page 20
for some tips on grilling
bread)

A generous pour of fancy olive
oil, to serve

Serves 4 to 6

Margot Henderson serves terrific brandade, the classic salt cod–potato mash that is as comforting as a cozy blanket by the fire. I'm inspired by her version, but I like to make my own salted cod. I prefer the texture to the boxed salt cod, and I can also control the sourcing of the fish this way, too. With commercial salt cod, you soak it for a couple of days, changing the water occasionally to rehydrate the fish and suck out the excess salt. I find it easier to start with fresh cod and salt that for a couple of hours before poaching. Everything turns out super-silky, and it's not a multiday investment. Brandade is great as is with grilled bread, but the mixture can also be chilled and rewarmed in the oven with an ample coating of grated Parmigiano or spread on toast and broiled with cheese.

In a medium saucepan, cover the salt cod in cold water and toss in the bay leaf, thyme sprigs, and half a lemon. Bring to a boil over high heat and then reduce the heat to a soft simmer and cook until the cod is cooked through and still tender, about 8 minutes. Pull the fish out of the water to cool.

In a medium saucepan, cover the potatoes with cold water and add 1 teaspoon salt. Bring to a boil, and then reduce the heat to a simmer. Cook until the potatoes are tender and easily mashed, about 20 to 25 minutes. Drain the potatoes very well, then mash them with a masher, or for a smoother puree, with a ricer. In a small saucepan over very low heat, combine the olive oil and smashed garlic and cook for 5 minutes. Remove the garlic when it begins to brown and is soft. Squeeze the remaining 1½ lemons into the olive oil. Stir in the milk. Keep at a slow simmer while preparing the fish.

Place the fish in a food processor and buzz to make a smooth paste, scraping the sides of the bowl occasionally. Gradually add about three-quarters of the milk-oil combination, reserving the rest to adjust texture later.

Scrape the fish mixture into a large bowl and fold in the mashed potatoes. Add more of the remaining milk mixture if necessary—the texture should be thick but spreadable. At this point, taste and adjust the seasoning with more salt, pepper, or lemon.

Serve warm with grilled bread and fancy olive oil.

scallops with 'nduja

Italian food is so special in London. Many Londoners spend holidays in the warmth of the Mediterranean, and hundreds of thousands of Italians have made London their home. The influence of the more than thirty-years-old River Café, with its emphasis on seasonal Italian dishes, is so strong among contemporary London restaurants, too: Basically, Italian simplicity marries beautifully with the good farm products of the English countryside. Luca is a more recent British-Italian destination, and I'm a little smitten. It's a big, ambitious space, and yet has all these intimate little nooks. The food is beautifully whittled down and sumptuous. At Luca, sea scallops arrive baked in their beautiful shells with a bit of spicy soft 'nduja sausage. If you can get your hands on scallop shells, by all means use them! If not, a pretty, simple plate will do just fine.

---

1 pound (455 g) dry-pack large scallops
Salt
½ cup (1 stick/115 g) unsalted butter
5 ounces (140 g) 'nduja sausage (I recommend La Quercia, a US-based maker of artisan cured meats made from heritage breeds), pulled into small pieces
1 tablespoon olive oil
1 lime, half for squeezing, half in wedges, to serve
Crunchy sea salt, to finish

Serves 2 to 4

Set the scallops out on a paper towel to dry. Season lightly with salt on both sides.

In a small sauté pan over medium heat, melt 4 tablespoons (55 g) of the butter, then add the 'nduja and break up the meat with the end of a spatula to make the sausage melt into the butter. When incorporated, turn off the heat and reserve.

Heat a 12- to 14-inch (30.5- to 35.5-cm) heavy steel pan over medium-high heat. Add the olive oil and 3 tablespoons of the butter to the pan and let melt. Pat each scallop top with a paper towel to dry the surface. When the butter is bubbling, place each scallop in the pan, making sure to not crowd the scallops together. Increase the heat to high and do not move the scallops. Let them cook for 1½ to 2 minutes, or until each has a nice dark caramel color. Flip each scallop with tongs and add one more tablespoon of butter to the pan. Squeeze about 1 tablespoon of lime juice into the pan and cook for another minute, basting the scallops using a large spoon. Cook until the scallops are just firm to touch and warm at their centers (use a knife to check one). They should be rare, but not cold, and should look raw and transparent at their centers.

When the scallops are done, place them on a warm plate. Reheat the 'nduja butter, about 30 seconds, and spoon over the scallops. Sprinkle with crunchy salt and serve with another wedge of lime to squeeze over.

ham with piccalilli

1 (4- to 5-pound/1.8- to
    2.3-kg) "city," or fully
    cooked, smoked ham cap
2 tablespoons brown sugar
3 tablespoons honey
3 tablespoons prepared
    English mustard
Piccalilli (page 339)

Serves 8 to 10

On one late-spring visit to the Maltby Street Market, I ran into a ham-slicing competition. About five competitors stood under awnings and raced to see who could most skillfully but quickly shave an entire bone-in leg of Spanish *jamon serrano*. It was hot, and the contestants and the ham slices alike looked overheated. I slipped into the coolness of 40 Maltby Street and had a much more British-feeling ham: a couple of slices of rosy baked ham with curried mustard as a complement. It reminded me how much I love British condiments, especially those with curry spices, like the mustard, and piccalilli, which is golden yellow and packed with chunky vegetables. It's perfect with any ham, but also roast chicken or a hearty cheese sandwich.

Heat the oven to 300°F (150°C). Place a kettle of water on to boil. Lightly score a crosshatch pattern into the top skin and fat of the ham, making sure to stop before hitting the meat.

In a small bowl, whisk together the sugar, honey, and mustard.

Place a rack in the bottom of a roasting pan. Pour enough boiling water into the pan to come up almost to the bottom of the rack. Place the ham on the rack and make sure it is not sitting in the water. Roast for 45 minutes, uncovered. Baste the ham with the honey glaze and continue roasting, basting every 30 minutes or so, about 2½ to 3 more hours, or until the ham is burnished and the interior temperature is above 140°F (60°C). Remove from the oven and let rest at least 30 minutes.

Slice the ham into fat slices and serve with piccalilli.

pork chops with roasted cherry tomatoes and pickled green tomatoes

1 (14 ounce/400 g or so) big, very high-quality pork chop, removed from the refrigerator 30 minutes before cooking

Salt

3 tablespoons olive oil

3 tablespoons unsalted butter

2 sprigs thyme

1 batch roasted cherry tomatoes (see page 48), cooled to room temperature

Pickled Green Tomatoes (page 340), at room temperature, to garnish

Serves 2 to 4

There's a presumption of farm-iness in many London restaurants that makes me chuckle and also kind of impresses me. Take Marksman Public House, the new-school pub restaurant noted for its love of British agriculture, where a pork chop was called simply "Roast Tamworth." Tamworth is a very old British breed of ginger-haired pig, and the chop we were served was monumental—and succulent, too, with bubbly, crisp skin. Sides were plainspoken—just perfect roast potatoes and a cozy brown blob of homemade apple "ketchup." If you serve a big chop like that to an individual, it's dinner, but if you roast it up and put it in the middle of the table, it becomes something a little more nibbly and interactive, especially with two forms of tomatoes to accent it: roasted cherries *and* green tomatoes all pickled up. (You'll want to make the pickles at least three days in advance.)

Heat the oven to 450°F (230°C).

Heat a heavy steel-bottomed skillet over medium-high heat. Season the pork chop on all sides with salt. Add the olive oil to the pan and carefully place the pork chop in the hot oil, shaking the pan gently while placing it to prevent sticking. Cook on one side, occasionally pressing down on the chop with a spatula to encourage a good crust. Cook for about 2½ minutes; before the oil begins to smoke, reduce the heat to medium-low. After 1 more minute, flip the chop and press down. Let cook for about 2 more minutes, then add the butter and thyme to the pan. Cook another 3 to 4 minutes, and then start spooning the butter over the pork chop. If the thick edge of the chop is still pale and rare, stand the chop on that edge to brown and render the fat. Cook until just pink at the interior, about 8 to 10 minutes total.

Remove from pan and let rest for at least 10 minutes. Serve with the roasted tomatoes and pickled tomatoes. Make sure to spoon some of the roasted tomato oil over the pork chops.

onion tart with lancashire cheese

4 tablespoons (55 g) unsalted
   butter
3 large yellow onions, thinly
   sliced
Salt
1 batch Pie Pastry
   (page 341)
All-purpose flour, for dusting
   and rolling
9 ounces (260 g) Lancashire
   cheese or white Cheddar,
   shredded
2 tablespoons milk, to seal
   the pie

Serves 6 to 8

Of course, England has a long tradition of savory pies, and they make so much sense for when your friends come over: You can just bake one ahead of time and plonk it down on the table, letting everyone serve themselves. Sebastian Delamothe, who was then a cheesemonger at Neal's Yard Dairy, suggested I try this tart, which calls out for a good ale and a big bowl of apples nearby.

Heat the oven to 325°F (170°C).

In a large saucepan or Dutch oven over medium heat, melt the butter, then add the onions. Season with about 1 teaspoon of salt and stir well. Cook slowly, until the onions are translucent and tender but not browned, about 15 to 20 minutes. Let cool, taste, and add more salt, remembering the cheese is somewhat salty as well.

Roll out half the dough and lay it into a deep tart tin with a removable base, at least 2 inches (5 cm) deep and 10 inches (25 cm) wide. Chill in the refrigerator for 10 minutes before filling. Sprinkle the bottom of the tart shell with a light layer of flour, about a teaspoon. Place about one-third of the cooled cooked onions in the bottom of the tart pan. Sprinkle half the cheese atop the onions. Place the next third of the cooked onions across the cheese. Sprinkle on the remaining cheese. Finally, place the remaining onions atop the cheese layer. Place in the refrigerator until ready to proceed.

Roll out the other half of the dough to an 11-inch (28-cm) round and chill for 10 minutes. Brush the top edge of the tart shell with some of the milk. Use a rolling pin to transport the disc of dough to the top of the tart shell, covering the cheese and onion filling. Push the dough lid into the lower tart shell, using a finger to pinch and seal the two crusts while trimming off any excess dough at the same time. Patch any holes with dough remnants. Cut a few slits in the pie top for venting. Brush the top of the tart with the remaining milk.

Bake for 1 hour and 20 minutes, or until light golden brown. Let cool for 30 minutes, then remove the outer ring of the tart pan. Let cool completely and serve the same day.

roast chicken salad, green beans, fennel, potatoes, and grainy dijon vinaigrette

1 whole chicken (about
4 pounds/1.8 kg)
2 tablespoons olive oil, plus
more to taste
2 teaspoons salt, plus more to
taste
1 pound (455 g) green beans,
trimmed
1 pound (455 g) small yellow
potatoes, scrubbed and
cut in half
1 batch Grainy Dijon
Vinaigrette (page 337)
2 small fennel bulbs, trimmed
and slivered on a
mandolin, about 2 cups
(180 g)
Freshly ground black pepper
Juice of ½ lemon, to finish

Serves 6 to 8

This salad is a riff on a dish I ate at Rochelle Canteen: a chicken salad with the veggies and potatoes all mixed together. Why keep everything isolated, when they can all be steeping in a sharp, grainy mustard dressing? I've included instructions for roasting the chicken, but if you've got a favorite rotisserie place or just some leftovers, feel free to use that instead.

Heat the oven to 450°F (230°C).

Rub the chicken with the 2 tablespoons olive oil and then season with 2 teaspoons salt. Place the chicken breast side up on a sturdy rimmed baking sheet or in a roasting pan and roast for 30 minutes. Reduce the temperature to 375°F (190°C) and cook 20 to 30 more minutes, until the temperature reads 165°F (75°C) at the thickest part of the thigh. Remove from the oven and let cool. When cool enough to touch, pull the meat into bite-size chunks, saving the skin and bones for making stock. Chill until ready to use (can be done the day before serving).

Have ready a large bowl of ice water. Bring a large pot of salted water to a boil. Drop in the green beans, let the water return to a boil, and then cook the beans until they are sweet and tender but still crisp, about 1 minute. Transfer the cooked beans to the ice bath to cool quickly. When cool, drain well and place in a large salad bowl.

Place the potatoes in a large pot and cover with about 2 inches (5 cm) of salted water. Bring the potatoes to a boil, then reduce the heat to a simmer. Cook until the potatoes are tender when pierced with a paring knife, about 20 minutes. Drain, then let the potatoes cool to lukewarm and place in the salad bowl with the beans.

Add the chicken chunks and toss with about two-thirds of the mustard vinaigrette. Add the fennel and toss, adding more vinaigrette, if desired. Taste and adjust the seasoning with additional salt, pepper, or a squeeze of lemon. Serve, piled high, on a stoneware platter.

The abundant shelves at Quality Wines, London

excellent british condiments

I don't know how I got out of Borough Market without a fifty-pound bag of jams, jellies, and chutneys. Traditional British cuisine is modest in seasoning: Sunday roasts and savory pastries don't typically get wild with the spices. But condiments are a different story. British colonization and commerce brought a world of spices and tropical ingredients such as citrus into the British pantry, which married well with the farmstead practices of pickling and preserving. The British pantry is filled with so many amazing accents that, fortunately, we can get our hands on easily these days. These condiments are the kinds of things that can turn a very plain dinner—roast chicken, a grilled cheese sandwich, a hard-cooked egg—into something pretty special. As much as I like making condiments myself, I also love having a pantry stocked with delicious ready-to-go jams and pickles. Look for great British preserving brands like Rosebud Preserves, from Yorkshire, in specialty stores and online.

Vivid yellow and sharp with mustard, piccalilli, the British take on South Asian pickles, has been a part of the British cooking vocabulary since at least the eighteenth century. I like it chunky with cauliflower, cucumber, and onion: It's almost as much a salad as it is a pickle. But there are other traditional pickled mixes, too. For instance, Branston pickle, a favorite accent for a ploughman's lunch of cheese and bread (and maybe an apple or ham), is a sweeter, more medieval-tasting pickle, with sweet spices and dates in the mix, that pairs perfectly with a sharp Cheddar.

Marmalades are among my favorite preserves. If I haven't made my own, I alternate between craving the lovely fine-cut version, which is perfect for brown-bread toast, and the super-chunky bitter versions, which stand their ground well alongside a hunk of Stilton.

In the spirit of marmalades, I like a jam that has some texture, too, though there may be such a thing as too much texture. I got the most delicious damson plum jam at the Borough market, and I almost lost a tooth: Turns out that the jam was so straight-from-the-orchard rustic that all the pits were in it! It was worth the risk, though—just delicious. In general, I look for slightly more obscure fruits in a British preserve—we have plenty of raspberry jam-makers here in the Pacific Northwest, but medlar, crabapple, gooseberry, and those damn stone-ridden damsons? Those are harder to find around here. You can almost never go wrong serving sweet-tart preserves next to a cheese or a country pâté.

baja

spicy beer, fish tacos, and crackling tostadas

If you're from the Northwest like me, you learn to live with the gray, dark winters. It's part of the rhythm of the year—you jam all your sunshine into the summer months, practically living outside, and then use the winter to catch up on stew-making, reading, and snuggling with your dog on the couch. It's the Seattle way.

That said, it doesn't hurt to make room for a little winter sunshine. A good dose of balmy weather can help you find equilibrium as the dreariness drags on and on.

Recently, Baja California—that long, skinny peninsula on the western edge of Mexico—has become my winter recharge of choice. I

love the landscape of desert scrub dotted with tall cacti raising their many arms to the sky. Bunnies dash by, and the prickly pears bloom hot pink against the tawny sand. Bougainvillea hang down from garden walls in shades of fuchsia, coral, and white. At night the uncountable stars arch across the velvety sky.

On one trip, we stood on the deck of a rental house watching the Super Blood Wolf Moon lunar eclipse. As a shadow crept across the moon, it transformed from a glowing orb to a pale coral marble, hanging heavily in the sky. A few neighbor dogs woofed in the night just to drive the point home.

Dan and I first went to Baja California a few years ago, when I was invited to cook at Rancho Pescadero, a resort built around an organic garden (which at this writing is currently closed for renovations—hopefully reopened by the time you read this). It was there that I sparked a new friendship with Dano Sanchez. You'll hear a lot about him later in this chapter. I'd been scared off by the overdevelopment at the end of the Baja peninsula, but here, an hour from Cabo, the towns are small and quiet and the landscape spectacular.

I've since gone back many times. I have cooked in my friends Drew and Paulina Deckman's outdoor restaurant in Mexico's premier wine region, Valle de Guadalupe, high in the mountains in the north of Baja. I've gone to eat at the famous seafood meccas in the big fishing town of Ensenada (and frankly seen some offshore fish-farming operations that really upset me there). I've gotten to know the pioneering Tijuana-raised chef Javier Plascencia.

The thing that keeps pulling me back, besides the sunshine, of course, are my growing friendships in the region and the West Coast ease I recognize from my life in Washington. Seafood here is treated with a casual respect: not too fussed with, but fresh and vibrant with accents of lime, chile, and tons of green herbs.

Back home, thinking about Baja points me in the direction of great seafood, raw or cooked, tweaked with just a couple of bright accents. It pushes me to explore the spectrum of chiles, from searing habanero heat to the mellow leather-and-plum flavors of guajillos. Even if there are a few months left before the summer sun arrives, I can grasp a little of the Tropic-of-Cancer feeling with recipes like these.

jalapeño and cilantro mezcal margarita

Lime wedges, to coat rims and garnish
Guajillo Chile Salt (page 337) or Tajín, spread out on a small plate
3 ounces (90 ml) mezcal
2 ounces (60 ml) Cilantro-Jalapeño Simple Syrup (page 336)
1½ ounces (40 ml) freshly squeezed lime juice
Cilantro sprigs, to garnish

Makes 2 cocktails

I'm always looking for a little something savory in my cocktails, so I like to swap the sweet orange liqueur called for in many margarita recipes with an herbaceous syrup made with green peppers and cilantro. Mixed with soda water and a good squeeze of lime, the syrup also makes a great non-alcoholic drink.

Moisten the rims of two cocktail glasses with a lime wedge. Dip the rims into the guajillo chile salt to coat. Fill each glass halfway with ice.

In a cocktail shaker or glass, stir together the mezcal, cilantro-jalapeño simple syrup, and lime juice. Pour the mixture into the prepared glasses and garnish each with a lime wedge and a few sprigs of cilantro.

paloma with rosemary

1 lime wedge
Kosher or crunchy sea salt, or Guajillo Chile Salt (page 337), spread out on a small plate
¼ cup (60 ml) grapefruit juice
1 teaspoon sugar
1 tablespoon lime juice
2 ounces (60 ml) mezcal or tequila
¼ cup (60 ml) soda water
1 pretty spear rosemary, to garnish
1 thin, semicircular slice of grapefruit (make sure to slice this before juicing the rest of the fruit)

Makes 1 cocktail

The paloma is an undersung cocktail of Mexico. Grapefruit and agave spirits taste so great together, I had to give you two drinks with the combination in this chapter. In bars, palomas are often made quickly with a grapefruit soda, but to get the right succulence, you need fresh-squeezed juice, like my friend Dano Sanchez uses at his idyllic Baja beach bar, Barracuda Cantina. Try his trick of garnishing with rosemary—its piney fragrance accents the drink so nicely.

Moisten the rim of a rocks glass with the lime wedge. Dip the rim into the salt to coat.

Pour in the grapefruit juice, sugar, lime juice, and mezcal and stir until the sugar is dissolved. Add lots of ice and top with the soda water. Garnish with the rosemary and grapefruit slice.

Jalapeño and Cilantro
Mezcal Margarita

dano's negroni

Lime wedges, to coat rims and
garnish
Guajillo Chile Salt
(page 337) or Tajín,
spread out on a small
plate
4 ounces (120 ml) joven
mezcal
3 ounces (90 ml) Hibiscus Tea
(page 338), cooled
2 ounces (60 ml) Aperol
1 ounce (30 ml) agave nectar
1½ ounces (45 ml) lime juice
Edible flowers, such as
blooming pineapple sage
(optional)

Makes 2 cocktails

Negronis made with mezcal instead of gin have become a
hit—I saw them called "mezconis" in Roman cocktail bars.
No thank you to the name, but agave spirits taste great with
bitters, and I love the way Dano worked another traditional
product, ruby red and tart hibiscus, or *jamaica*, into his version of the drink.

Moisten the rims of two cocktail glasses with a lime wedge.
Dip the rims into the guajillo chile salt to coat. Fill each glass
halfway with ice. In a cocktail shaker, combine the mezcal,
tea, Aperol, agave, and lime juice. Add ice and shake vigorously. Strain into the prepared glasses and garnish with
lime wedges and edible flowers, if desired.

tocayo's mezcal and tonic

4 ounces (120 ml) mezcal
Grapefruit bitters
1 small red grapefruit, cut into
8 wedges
2 small (6.8 ounces/200 ml)
bottles chilled tonic water

Makes 4 cocktails

Since they share a name, Dano calls my husband, Dan, *tocayo*,
or namesake. This combination has become my Dan's signature summer drink, and he makes it by the trayful. It turns
out tonic isn't just great with gin—mixed with savory mezcal
and layers of grapefruit, it makes a kind of renegade paloma
that's so refreshing in the heat.

In each of four glasses, place 3 to 4 ice cubes, followed by
1 ounce (30 ml) mezcal, a dash of grapefruit bitters, and a
squeeze of juice from a grapefruit wedge. Fill each glass with
tonic and garnish with a wedge of grapefruit.

Dano's Negroni

the barracuda

Lime wedges, to coat rims and
garnish
Guajillo Chile Salt
(page 337) or Tajín,
spread out on a small
plate
4 ounces (120 ml) joven
mezcal
1½ ounces (40 ml) Ancho
Reyes Verde
4 basil leaves, plus 2 small
sprigs, to garnish
1 ounce (30 ml) lime juice
½ ounce (15 ml) agave nectar
Pulp from 2 ripe passion fruits,
about 4 ounces (120 ml)

Makes 2 cocktails

Ancho Reyes Verde is a liqueur made with green poblano chiles that adds sweetness and savoriness to a cocktail—it's a dynamite partner to passion fruit, like the ones that grow in the courtyard of Dano's bar, Barracuda Cantina.

Moisten the rims of two cocktail glasses with a lime wedge. Dip the rims into the guajillo chile salt to coat. Fill each glass halfway with ice.

In a cocktail shaker, combine the mezcal, liqueur, basil, lime juice, agave nectar, and passion fruit. Add ice and shake vigorously. Strain through a fine-mesh strainer and divide the cocktail between the two glasses. Garnish each with a basil sprig and lime wedge.

Dano Sanchez, master bartender and friend

spirit of the agave

In Mexico, authenticity can come in a plastic 2-liter Coke bottle. There's a special pride in mezcal so artisanal that it has never been bottled in glass, but simply toted around in a reused plastic container. Dano showed up to our little cocktail party with an old soda bottle filled with aromatic mezcal from Oaxaca. There's no label, but when he bought it, he got to see a Polaroid photo of the maker, Tomas.

Dano, who has a beautiful tattoo of the spiked agave plant on his arm, is dedicated to the spirit made from it. "I love the flavor, I love the way it makes me feel. I fell in love with the mysticism of the plant." Agave has been a sacred plant in Mexico for centuries, and the goddess of the plant, Mayahuel, was worshiped by the Aztecs. The tradition and patience needed to make mezcal is part of its appeal. Dano reminds, "It takes ten rainy seasons, ten summers, ten winters for a plant to finalize the circle of life—to finally be harvested and become Mayahuel's spirit."

Unrecognized in the United States a couple of decades ago, mezcal is having an explosive moment. Big companies are getting into the game, which used to be chiefly the stuff of the Tomases of the world. But if you're not already knee-deep in the cocktail scene, it can be confusing to sort through countless agave spirits.

Tequila is actually a form of mezcal. It's made with one kind of agave—blue agave, most famously in the state of Jalisco, though it can also be made in areas of Michoacán, Guanajuato, Nayarit, and Tamaulipas. It can be a wonderful spirit, of course, but the international attention and huge sales mean that tequila production tends to be more high-volume and less quirky than that of other agave spirits.

When an agave plant is ready for mezcal production, it is removed from the ground and its spiky leaves are trimmed, leaving behind the *piña*, or agave heart. The piñas are then roasted underground—the source of the smokiness that many mezcals possess (tequila is usually made with hearts steamed in copper instead). The agave hearts are then ground, by hand or machine. Traditional mezcal is often distilled in clay pots, not the high-efficiency stills of higher production facilities.

For a long time, non-tequila mezcal had very little export potential. Mezcal was produced for regional, even village-level, consumption, including ceremonial and medicinal uses. Its status as an indigenous drink also meant it was undervalued by Mexicans of European origin and visitors alike. Mezcal can be made with many varietals of agave, and in many different regions, including Durango, Guanajuato, Guerrero, San Luis Potosí, Tamaulipas, Zacatecas, Michoacán, Puebla, and, most famously, Oaxaca. In the past couple of decades, consumers around the world have embraced mezcal specifically because of these eclectic differences, and there is a huge and growing market for mezcal for export.

This growth is tricky to manage: How do you expand while still holding on to the specific characteristics of small, local production? Fourth-generation mezcal maker Graciela Angeles Carreño of Real Minero, who gave me a tour of her family's operation, is striving to combine sustainable growth with the traditional methods that make mezcal so distinctive. Real Minero is growing an agave nursery from seed with a variety of agaves, experimenting with natural pesticides, and also planting trees that are traditionally harvested for

cooking agave. I am proud that the Real Minero mezcals we sell in our restaurant support her agricultural conservancy work.

Young mezcal is called *joven*, and like *plata tequila*, it is what you would most commonly mix into a cocktail, since its herbaceous, bright, agave-forward nature tastes so good with other flavors. As the spirits spend more time in barrels, they get more golden and weightier in flavor. *Reposados* of mezcal or tequila—barreled for more than two months but less than a year—have a golden tone and some oak flavors, while *añejos*—aged between one and three years in oak—have even more caramel tones.

Because of the range of production methods, agave varietals, and terroir, mezcal takes a while to get to know. It can be airy, floral, and crystalline, or it can out-smoke the peatiest Scotch whisky.

This variation is part of the pleasure of mezcal. The best way to further your education is to go to a bar that specializes in mezcal and sip them side by side. In Todos Santos, there's a mezcaleria called El Refugio that also serves a few classic dishes from the kitchen each night—excellent fish in salsa poblano, for example. They feature small family producers working with the most traditional methods, and each mezcal has its own story to tell. And those stories are as vivid and overheated as a telenovela. One Espadín mezcal was described as "as solid as a satisfying Facebook rant," and another "like tracking a satyr though Norwegian wood."

I'm not sure I'm that sensitive (or flamboyant!) of a taster of mezcal. I like to keep just a couple of bottles at home for sipping or for mixing. Del Maguey Vida is a great option for a citrusy, herbaceous spirit, and then Fidencio Joven Clasico offers a luscious smoky taste without being overwhelming. As for tequila, for cocktails, I love the crisp taste of a white or plata, like Arette or Tequila Ocho.

toasted peanuts
with chile and lime

3 cups (450 g) raw, unsalted
    peanuts
¼ cup (60 ml) lime juice (from
    about 2 large limes)
2 teaspoons salt
1 teaspoon hot smoked
    paprika
1 teaspoon chipotle chile
    powder

Makes 3 cups (315 g)

So simple, so good. The lime and chile on the surface of these peanuts echoes the tangy spice of addictive Tajín seasoning. You'll find yourself tossing these on salads and on veggies, and, of course, just scooping them up by the handful.

Heat the oven to 325°F (170°C).

Spread the peanuts out on a baking sheet and toast until fragrant and light golden brown, about 6 to 7 minutes. Shake the pan at least once during toasting.

Remove the peanuts from the oven but keep the oven on. Transfer the hot peanuts to a large bowl, then add the lime juice, salt, paprika, and chile powder and toss to coat evenly. Once the peanuts are well seasoned, pour them back onto the baking sheet and return to the oven. Cook about 5 minutes, stirring occasionally, and remove from the oven once the nuts are well-dried. Remove and let cool to room temperature on the baking sheet. Check salt one last time—add a little more if necessary—and serve. The peanuts will keep in a sealed container at room temperature for up to a week.

i love chips!

In Mexico, you don't have to go far to find good tortillas or chips. Even small-town convenience stores keep Coleman chests loaded with parcels of fresh, still-warm tortillas, and there are thick, shatteringly crisp *totopos* (thick-cut tortilla chips) on the shelves.

But it's harder to find good masa products stateside. Of course, you should seek out a local Latin market, but it's fun to fry your own, and there is nothing better than a warm, crisp chip. Here's the basic method, but feel free to play around with tortilla type (blue corn, yellow corn, etc.) and the shapes you decide to fry.

Have ready a spider or a slotted spoon and a baking sheet fitted with a wire cooling rack or a double layer of paper towels, which you will need to change frequently. In a large cast-iron pot or Dutch oven, heat 3 inches (7.5 cm) of neutral oil, such as grapeseed, over medium heat to 350°F (180°C).

Cut your tortillas in the shape you desire—wedges are great, but so are fat strips. Fry the chips about six to eight at a time for 1 minute. Give them a gentle stir with your spoon or spider partway through the fry. Keep checking the temperature, otherwise they may burn or be greasy and not cooked enough. Scoop out and drain on paper towels. Salt right away.

Eat as soon as you can with salsa, smashed avocado, and a cold beer rimmed with chile salt and lime.

tomatillo and avocado salsa

12 tomatillos, husks removed
1 small ripe avocado, halved,
    pitted, and peeled
½ bunch cilantro, leaves and
    stems included (about
    2 cups/80 g)
Zest and juice from
    2 small limes (about
    3 tablespoons juice)
1 serrano chile, stem removed
Salt

Makes about 1 cup (240 ml)

This green salsa, smoothed with a bit of avocado, is a classic accent for seafood all over the peninsula, including the delicious fish and shrimp tacos at Barracuda. It's great with chips, of course, but I love it as a sauce for fried silver fish, as a ceviche marinade, or with batter-fried jalapeños.

In a large heavy skillet over medium-high heat, cook the tomatillos until charred on one side, about 5 minutes. Turn the tomatillos and continue cooking until they are browned on most surfaces and softening, another 10 to 12 minutes. Slip the tomatillos into a bowl and cover with a plate. Let steam for 10 minutes, then place the tomatillos in a blender with the avocado, cilantro, lime zest and juice, serrano, and ½ teaspoon salt. Buzz until very smooth. Taste and season with more salt or lime juice, if desired.

Store in an airtight jar in the refrigerator until ready to eat. It will keep well for 2 to 3 days.

salsa macha

1½ cups (360 ml) olive oil
4 garlic cloves, peeled
1 cup (105 g) toasted skinless peanuts (see page 248)
6 ounces (175 g) dried guajillo chiles, about 15 large chiles, seeds
    removed, cut into strips
¼ cup (40 g) untoasted sesame seeds
1 teaspoon salt
¼ cup (60 ml) lime juice, from about 2 large limes

Makes about 3 cups (710 ml)

Salsa macha is a Veracruz specialty—fragrant chiles confited in oil with garlic and peanuts and sesame—but it's become a favorite table condiment around different parts of Mexico, including Baja, I think, because its richness works so well in contrast to other sharper salsas. I first came across it at a great little seafood place in Oaxaca called Sirilo, where it was served with a raw tuna dish. It was fantastic: savory and lingering against the clean, bright fish. This recipe makes a good amount because it keeps well—at least a week in the refrigerator—and you'll want to use it on everything: fish, chicken, eggs, and just scooped up on thick tortilla chips.

In a 3- to 4-inch (7.5- to 10-cm) heavy cast-iron or enameled saucepan over medium-high, heat the oil and garlic for 3 to 4 minutes. Add half the peanuts and cook for 30 seconds, stirring the whole time. Then add the chiles, stir, and remove from the heat. Let the mixture steep, stirring and turning the chiles every 3 minutes or so, until cooled, about 1 hour.

When the mixture has cooled completely, place it in a blender, working in batches if necessary. Blend until the chiles and peanuts are in very small bits but not totally emulsified. Add the remaining peanuts and pulse for a few seconds so that there are some larger chunks of peanuts. Add the sesame seeds, salt, and lime juice. Pulse briefly to incorporate, and then use right away or store in an airtight jar in the refrigerator until ready to use.

smashed avocado with slivered jalapeño and chips

5 small ripe avocados, halved and pitted

1 tablespoon lime juice

1½ teaspoons kosher salt, plus more to taste

½ jalapeño pepper, very thinly sliced

2 tablespoons roughly chopped cilantro, to garnish

Crunchy sea salt, to finish

Pinch of chipotle powder, to garnish

1 tablespoon (or more) olive oil, to garnish

Lime wedges, to serve

Chips (preferably fat totopos; see page 251 to make your own), to serve

Serves 6

Guacamole is my mom's favorite food in the world, and we had it a lot when I was growing up—usually with good-ol' hard-shell tacos (filled with ground beef and iceberg lettuce, naturally!). She would always line the avocados up on a plate and smash them up with a fork before seasoning them. I still love guacamole, and I make it a little differently every time, mixing in finely minced onion, or tossing some coriander flowers on top, if I've got them in the garden. But this version, with thinly slivered chiles and a decadent drizzle of olive oil, is stripped-down and gorgeous. I don't like it when the guac is too smooth, so I leave some big chunks to grab with your chips.

You can use my mother's method, smashing the avocados with a fork on a plate, but I work over a medium mixing bowl and chop into each avocado half with a spoon, then scoop it into the bowl. Add the lime juice and salt, and mix and mash the avocado, blending well but keeping it chunky. Taste and adjust the seasoning with more salt or lime if necessary.

Fold in the jalapeño to evenly distribute it, and transfer to a serving dish. Sprinkle with cilantro, crunchy salt, and chipotle powder. Drizzle with olive oil and serve with lime wedges and chips.

clam ceviche with serrano and cilantro

2½ cups (600 ml) shucked
and coarsely chopped
clam meat (from about
3 pounds/1.4 kg Manila
clams or 12 blood clams)

3 garlic cloves, grated

2 teaspoons minced seeded
serrano chile, plus more
to taste

½ small white onion, minced

Juice of 4 limes, about ½ cup
(120 ml) lime juice, plus
more to taste

¼ cup (60 ml) olive oil

½ cup (20 g) minced cilantro
stems and leaves

½ teaspoon salt, plus more to
taste

Saltines, to serve

Serves 6

In Baja, Dano helped us get a hold of palm-size clams called chocolate clams or, less invitingly, blood clams. Their name comes from their flaming coral feet (the tongue-like part that sticks out of the shell). They are mellow with a gentle brine. Since you may not be able to get those pretty clams in your neighborhood, you will do well with more easily found clams like Manilas. While I shuck large clams like his raw, doing the same for small clams is a tedious business, so you can steam them quickly instead (see Note).

In a medium bowl, toss together the clam meat, garlic, serrano, onion, lime juice, olive oil, cilantro, and salt. Taste and adjust the seasoning with additional salt, serrano, or lime juice, if desired.

You can let it sit for a bit in the refrigerator, if you make it in advance, or you can serve this immediately with the saltines.

Note: Shucking and Steaming Clams

To shuck large clams: Holding the clam at the hinge, slide a thin knife along the upper shell to detach the scallop-like adductor muscles from its anchor points on either side of the top shell. Pull out the clam and, using scissors, remove the soft belly and discard it. You will be left with the tongue-shaped foot, the adductors, and the ring of flexible mantle. Place these in the bowl as you shuck the remaining clams. If cooking the meat, hold on to the shells.

To shuck small clams: Small Manila clams, the kind I work with most frequently in the Northwest, are a bear to shuck, so I steam them very briefly to get their meat. Heat a wide skillet or braising pan with a lid over medium high-heat and add 2 tablespoons olive oil. Add the clams and ¼ cup (60 ml) water and cover immediately. Shake and cook for 2 minutes. Peek in every so often and remove each clam with tongs as soon as it opens so it remains soft and tender. Discard any clam that does not open 5 minutes after the first ones pop open. Once cool enough to handle, pluck the clams from the shells and chill until ready to use.

rockfish ceviche with tomatillo and avocado salsa

Recipes like ceviche and aguachile were developed by generations of fishermen and their families, with the knowledge that seafood or near-raw seafood tastes magnificent when marinated in tangy big-flavored marinades. The salt, chile, and acid in the preparation would have helped preserve seafood so none of it was wasted. Preparing raw seafood may seem intimidating, but shop in a seafood market you trust and it's not too tricky. There is a bit of nuance, though: The longer the marinade sits on the fish, the more "cooked" it gets—the flesh will tighten and whiten up in the acid. You can decide how long you like; I prefer to serve this when the fish is still silky and raw at the center of each bite, so I find 10 minutes is about right for this size of fish chunk.

Heat the oven to 400°F (200°C).

Brush the tortillas generously with olive oil and sprinkle with crunchy salt. Lay the tortillas in a single layer on two baking sheets. Bake for five minutes, flip the tortillas, then bake another 5 to 10 minutes, until the tostadas are crispy and brown. Once cooled, they can keep overnight in an airtight container.

In a medium bowl, combine the rockfish, ¾ cup (180 ml) tomatillo salsa, red onion, 1 tablespoon olive oil, lime juice, scallions, serrano, radishes, 1 tablespoon of the sesame seeds, and salt. Let sit for at least 10 minutes.

Scoop the ceviche into a serving bowl. Add a bit more salsa if you would like a juicier ceviche, garnish with cilantro, the remaining 1 tablespoon sesame seeds, and crunchy salt. Serve with tostadas.

10 corn tortillas (I like Three Sisters Nixtamal blue corn tortillas)
Olive oil
Crunchy sea salt
¾ pound (340 g) rockfish, skinned, boned, and diced into ½-inch (12-mm) cubes
¾ to 1 cup (180 to 240 ml) Tomatillo and Avocado Salsa (page 252)
½ red onion, thinly sliced
Juice from 1 lime, about 2 tablespoons
Greens from 2 scallions, sliced very thin on the bias
1 serrano chile, sliced very thin
3 radishes, thinly sliced
2 tablespoons toasted sesame seeds
Salt
Cilantro leaves, to garnish

Serves 4 to 6

beachside ease

On my most recent trip to Baja, my first stop was in Cerritos, a beach town just south of Todos Santos. We bumped along the rutted, unpaved road where several homes were in the midst of being built. At many of the beaches in the Todos Santos area, the waves crash hard right into the sand, but Cerritos is a beautiful break, and the camper vans and pickups parked along the road all carry surfboards. A few hundred yards from the beach is our friend Dano Sanchez's beach bar, Barracuda Cantina.

The cantina itself is a bar with a *palapa* roof over the sand, with several tiled tables hand-built by Dano and his friends. Across the lot is a bright-green taco truck, which turns out delicious fish tacos and seafood ceviche all day long. One of Dano's five rescue dogs, the French bulldog Queen Latifah, wandered among the tables, hoping for a dropped morsel of shrimp or yellowtail while stalking the cat that was hidden under the truck.

Dano—with his easy smile and bits of zinc sunscreen from his morning surf session still sticking to his cheeks—came out to greet us after our trip with not-so-small shots of mezcal and a plateful of *naranjitos* (a fruit kind of like a kumquat), sprinkled with chile and salt. We toasted and sucked on the sour aromatic fruit, and our trip had officially begun.

I met Dano a few years ago, when he was running the bar service at Rancho Pescadero, and we visited soon after he had opened the beach bar in 2017. He and his wife, Karla, also a veteran in the hospitality industry, are curious, extroverted, and proud of the little haven they have created beside the ocean that pulls together not just a bar and a food truck but also a garden.

For Karla, the relaxed vibe was hard-won. I was honored that she shared the story of coming to Baja from her home state of Chihuahua, where she had almost completed her communications degree at the university in Ciudad Juárez, a place that had (and still has) a horrifying record of femicide—the murder of hundreds of young women in the region and an accompanying lack of response from the authorities. In the city, Karla lived under a cloud of fear. When she first came to Todos Santos to visit her sister, easy-going Baja seemed strange at first. Ordinary events like gathering around a nighttime beach bonfire seemed wildly risky. But a few days in, the possibility of a life with less fear emerged, and she soon decided to move to Baja. Shortly thereafter, she met Dano, and they have been together since 2008.

Behind the tables, a passion fruit vine grows lushly, bearing big golden orbs much prettier than the muddy-colored ones we sometimes get up north. He's gathered a big load of them the morning of our visit, and he cracks one open to make one of his beautifully balanced drinks—a refreshing tonic of passion fruit, gently smoky mezcal, and Ancho Reyes, a liqueur made with leathery-sweet ancho chiles. Dano's drinks all deliver the fruity dream of a beachside drink, but without cloying sweetness—they all have a savory element. Many Mexican fruit stands offer mangos or melon sprinkled with chile lime and salt, and this drink has that same kind of balance.

There is so much good energy under that palm roof. Unfortunately I can't pack it and take it home with me, but I can still summon some of the Barracuda spirit in my own kitchen. It all starts with juicing limes, chopping chiles and cilantro, and maybe pouring a little glass of mezcal.

scallop and tomatillo aguachile

12 to 15 large tomatillos, husks removed

¼ cup (60 ml) lime juice

2 serrano chiles, 1 chopped, 1 thinly sliced

1 cup (40 g) packed cilantro leaves and stems

Fine sea salt

12 large dry-pack sea scallops, sliced into 3 or 4 thin rounds each

½ medium cucumber, thinly sliced

6 radishes, thinly sliced

Olive oil, to drizzle

Crunchy sea salt, to finish

Serves 6

Aguachile—literally, "chile water"—is a classic recipe from Sinaloa in the northwest of Mexico, and is typically made with raw shrimp and fresh chiles pureed with water. But the concept has traveled throughout the country. It's generally a juicier, spicier approach to ceviche and is regularly reinterpreted by modern Mexican chefs like Enrique Olvera and Gabriela Cámara.

Chill a serving bowl or platter.

Heat a heavy skillet over medium-high heat and place the tomatillos in it. Cook until well browned on one side (about 5 minutes), then turn the tomatillos and continue to brown on other sides, for about 10 more minutes.

Working in batches if necessary, in a blender, puree the tomatillos, ½ cup (120 ml) water, lime juice, chopped serrano, cilantro, and 1 teaspoon fine sea salt until smooth. Chill in the refrigerator until cold.

To assemble the aguachile, place a dollop of the tomatillo mixture in the bottom of the chilled bowl. Layer some of the scallop slices on top of the sauce, and season lightly with fine sea salt. Top each one with a bit more sauce. Add a layer of cucumber slices and salt very lightly. Lay a layer of radishes on top of the scallops and very lightly season them. Repeat the scallop, tomatillo sauce, cucumber, and radish layers, lightly seasoning each layer and finishing with a few slices of serranos on top. Drizzle the top layer with olive oil and season with crunchy sea salt.

shrimp cocktail with tomato and cilantro oil

1 cup (40 g) chopped cilantro stems

1 cup (240 ml) grapeseed or other neutral oil

2½ teaspoons salt, plus more to taste

½ teaspoon seeded and roughly chopped serrano chile, plus 1 serrano, very thinly sliced

30 shell-on wild Gulf shrimp, size 16–20

2 cans (24 ounces/720 ml total) of light-bodied lager, like Tecate

1 ancho chile

5 tablespoons (75 ml) lime juice, plus more to taste

1 medium tomato, cut into slim wedges

Saltine crackers, to serve

Serves 6

Mexican shrimp cocktail tends to be tomato-y and almost soupy. In this variation, I kept the juiciness while shifting the flavor to a vibrant cilantro puree. The shrimp are poached in a couple of cans of Mexican lager. I recommend picking up a six-pack, leaving you with a few extra beers to enjoy alongside the shrimp.

Bring 2 cups (480 ml) water to a boil in a small saucepan. Place the cilantro stems in the water and turn off the heat. After 30 seconds, drain the stems, then let cool. In a blender, combine the stems, oil, 1 teaspoon salt, and the roughly chopped serrano and puree until smooth. Strain through a fine-mesh sieve. Store the oil in an airtight jar in the refrigerator for up to a week.

If the shrimp have not been deveined, use a small knife to slice through the shell along their backs. Using tweezers or your fingers, devein the shrimp.

In a medium saucepan, bring the beer, ancho, 2 tablespoons lime juice, and 1 teaspoon salt to a boil. Reduce the heat to low and simmer for 15 minutes. Remove the chile and discard.

Bring the beer mixture to a boil again. Place half the shrimp in the liquid, reduce the heat to a simmer, and cook for 2 minutes. Using a slotted spoon or a spider, remove the shrimp, lay them out on a plate, and put them in the refrigerator to cool. Repeat with the remaining shrimp.

When the shrimp are cool, peel them and cut the shrimp in half lengthwise. In a large bowl, toss the shrimp with the tomato, about ½ cup (60 ml) of the cilantro oil, the remaining 3 tablespoons lime juice, and ½ teaspoon salt. Taste and adjust the seasoning with more cilantro oil, salt, or lime, if desired. Place in a large serving bowl or platter and garnish with the serrano slices. Serve with saltines.

tomato salad with salsa macha

Once I have some Salsa Macha—the rich, peanut-and-chile salsa—on hand, it ends up in everything; it's so good. Save this salad for summer, when you have the ripest tomatoes available. Unless, of course, you happen to be in Baja, when they are delicious midwinter, too!

½ cup (120 ml) Salsa Macha (page 255)
3 pounds (1.4 kg) perfect summer tomatoes, larger ones cut into big chunks, and cherries halved
Crunchy sea salt, to finish
3 to 4 tablespoons olive oil

Serves 6 to 8

In a large serving bowl, spoon big dollops of the salsa macha. Arrange some of the tomatoes on top, then spoon more salsa on top. Continue arranging, alternating with the remaining salsa and tomatoes.

Sprinkle with crunchy salt and drizzle with olive oil to add gloss and flavor.

goat cheese with honeycomb, chipotle, and salt

8 ounces (225 g) fresh goat
cheese—look for a cheese
with a high fat content
(or you can stir a few
tablespoons of cream into
it to richen it up)
2 tablespoons chipotle
powder
1 teaspoon crunchy sea salt
½ cup (120 ml) honey with
honeycomb
Charred tortillas or good thick
tortilla chips

Serves 4

At the organic fruit stand in Todos Santos, there were
gorgeous jars of local honey with the comb inside. Our
salesman wanted to make sure we ate the comb with a
mozzarella-like panela cheese, but instead, I found an almost
mascarpone-rich goat cheese. I knew it would taste great
with the honeycomb, especially with charred tortillas and a
smoky pinch of chipotle powder. I've tried again back home
with my favorite local fresh chèvre, and it's delicious, too.

Let the cheese warm to room temperature. Sprinkle with the
chipotle powder and crunchy salt. Serve with the honeycomb
next door on the plate, or in a little bowl, along with tortillas.

black beans with coriander, pickled onions, and crema

1½ cups (650 g) dry black
　　beans, soaked overnight
　　in cold water
½ white onion, peeled
3 garlic cloves, peeled
1 bay leaf
2½ teaspoons salt, plus more
　　to taste
¾ cup (80 ml) white wine
　　vinegar
1 red onion, cut into ¼-inch
　　(6-mm) slices
1 tablespoon coriander seeds
1 tablespoon cumin seeds
¼ cup (60 ml) olive oil
Juice of 2 small limes, plus
　　more to taste
½ cup (120 ml) crema or crème
　　fraîche
2 tablespoons chopped
　　cilantro leaves and stems,
　　plus flowers if you have
　　them
Crunchy sea salt, to finish

Serves 6 to 8

I love bean salads. They feel like the perfect do-ahead food, getting better over time. They are great at room temp, too; in fact, I prefer them this way. With beans, it is super important to have enough dressing to give the salad some forceful flavor. Here, the toasted spices help keep this salad bright and interesting over time. Feel free to change the black beans out for your favorite bean, and always double-check the seasoning just before serving, especially if you made the salad earlier in the day.

Drain the black beans and place them in a 3- to 4-quart (3- to 4-L) saucepan with the white onion, garlic, and bay leaf. Add enough water to cover the beans by 2 inches (5 cm). Bring to a boil, then reduce the heat to a gentle simmer. Cook for 20 minutes, then season with 1 teaspoon of the salt. Continue to cook until the beans are tender but not mushy, 10 to 20 more minutes, depending on the freshness of the beans. Drain, discard the onion, garlic, and bay leaf, then spread the beans out on a baking sheet and refrigerate to cool.

While the beans are cooking, bring ½ cup (120 ml) water, the vinegar, and ½ teaspoon of the salt to a boil. Add the red onion to the vinegar mixture, stir, and turn off the heat. Let cool to room temperature.

In a dry skillet over medium heat, toast the coriander and cumin seeds until fragrant. Let them cool, then coarsely grind or crush in a mortar and pestle.

In a large bowl, toss the cooled beans with the crushed spices, olive oil, lime juice, and 1 teaspoon of the salt. Season with more salt or lime juice, if desired.

Arrange the bean mixture in a serving dish and spoon the crema in large blobs on top. Drain some of the pickled onions and drape them on top of the crema. Finish the dish with a sprinkle of cilantro and crunchy salt.

squash blossom quesadillas

½ cup (200 g) thinly sliced zucchini (baby zucchini if available)

¼ teaspoon salt

1 tablespoon lime juice

4 (8-inch/20-cm) corn tortillas

2⅔ cups (320 g) shredded melting cheese, preferably queso asadero or queso Oaxaca

16 squash blossoms with stamens removed, plus more to garnish, if available

2 teaspoons olive oil, plus more for any extra blossoms

Fine sea salt

Serves 4

There's a time in the early summer when the farmers are thinning their crops and the markets are alight with trumpet-shaped squash blossoms. They look fancy, but they are actually simple to work with. They taste like slightly spicy zucchini, and they are so pretty peeking out from a tortilla blanket.

Toss the zucchini in a small bowl with the salt and lime juice. Set aside.

Cover half of each tortilla with about ⅓ cup (80 g) cheese. Lay 4 blossoms on top of the cheese with the petals facing the edge of the tortilla. Cover with ⅓ cup (80 g) cheese and fold the tortilla over. Repeat with the remaining tortillas.

Heat a cast-iron pan over medium heat. Drizzle 1 teaspoon oil into the pan and place two of the assembled tortillas in it. Cook until brown on one side, about 3 minutes, then flip to the other side and cook until well melted and crispy, about 3 or 4 more minutes. Repeat with the remaining quesadillas.

If you have extra blossoms, sauté them in a pan with a couple of teaspoons of olive oil. Cut the quesadillas into wedges and top with the salted zucchini and the extra sautéed blossoms.

guajillo grilled clams

2 cups (480 g) raw chopped
    clam meat, about
    12 chocolate or butter
    clams, or more for
    smaller clams (see Note,
    page 258, for how to
    shuck, and make sure to
    reserve the half shells)
¾ cup (180 ml) Salsa Macha
    (page 255)
2 tablespoons unsalted butter,
    divided into 12 pats
Lime wedges, to serve

Serves 4 to 6

Jazamango is an outdoor garden restaurant owned by my friend Javier Plascencia. My favorite dish there is the chocolate clams on the half shell that were cooked in the wood-fired oven. Here's my take, using more Salsa Macha—what can I say? It goes with everything!

Prepare a charcoal grill with a hot fire and place the grate on top.

In a bowl, combine the clam meat and the salsa, then spoon the mixture into the reserved shells. Place a pat of butter on each shell.

Have ready a serving dish heaped with rock salt or dried beans to hold the clamshells without losing their juices.

Grill the clams over the hottest coals until bubbly and browning on the edge, about 4 minutes.

Serve with lime wedges on the prepared plate.

charred onions with jalapeño crema

At roadside chicken stands, you're likely to get your chicken served with charred onions, cooked into submission until they are soft, steamy, and sweet inside. So simple and so good. I like to cook onions directly on the coals—it's earthy and elemental. This presentation dresses them up a bit, with a voluptuous, gently spiced jalapeño crema.

Prepare a charcoal grill with a hot fire and when the coals are ashed over, place the onions directly onto the gray coals. Cook, turning the onions occasionally, until they feel soft when squeezed with the tongs but don't totally collapse, about 15 to 20 minutes, depending on the size of the onion.

Pull the onions out of the fire into a large bowl, cover with a plate or a kitchen towel, and let them steam and cool to room temperature, about 30 minutes. When cool, remove the papery skins and cut the onions into chunks.

In a blender, combine the sour cream, 2 tablespoons of the olive oil, the jalapeños, serrano, 1 teaspoon salt, the avocado, cilantro, oregano, lime zest, and 3 tablespoons of the lime juice. Buzz until completely smooth. Taste and adjust the seasoning with more salt or lime juice if desired.

Spoon a thick layer of the crema on a serving platter, then arrange a layer of onions on top. Drape with more crema and then top with the remaining onions. Sprinkle the remaining lime juice over the onions, drizzle with the remaining olive oil, then garnish with the sesame seeds, crunchy salt, and the chipotle powder.

8 whole medium yellow
   onions, skin on
1 cup (240 ml) sour cream
4 tablespoons (60 ml) olive oil
2 jalapeños with seeds
   (remove the seeds if you
   want it less spicy)
1 serrano pepper, seeded
1 teaspoon salt, plus more
   to taste
½ ripe avocado
½ cup (20 g) packed cilantro
   stems and leaves
1 teaspoon dried oregano
Zest of 1 lime
5 tablespoons (75 ml) lime
   juice
3 tablespoons toasted sesame
   seeds
Crunchy sea salt, to finish
1 tablespoon chipotle chile
   powder

Serves 6 to 8

grilled chicken
with salsa roja and lime

1 cup (240 ml) Smooth
  Smoked Chile Salsa Roja
  (page 343)
1 chicken, about 3 pounds
  (1.4 kg), butchered into
  6 pieces (breasts, thighs,
  drumsticks)
1 tablespoon neutral cooking
  oil, such as grapeseed or
  canola
Salt
1 lime, cut into wedges
1 batch charred onions
  (see page 279)

Serves 4

Pollo asado stands pepper the roadsides in Baja and elsewhere in Mexico. Sometimes there's a masonry grill, and sometimes there's just a metal barrel cut open and coated with eye-catching paint. Either way, a well-grilled chicken is a thing of beauty. The smoky flavor of the chile rub mingles perfectly with the char of the grilling. If you already have the grill heated, you might like to also cook the charred onions from the previous page; their succulence is a great complement to the smoky chicken. Another great accent? A cool glass of Mina Penélope Amber from Valle de Guadalupe in northern Baja. Winemaker Veronica Santiago is making some of my favorite Mexican wines, and this orange rosé is crisp but rich enough with notes of honeysuckle and stone fruit to handle the spice in the salsa.

Rub the salsa roja all over the chicken pieces. Refrigerate the chicken for at least 6 hours or overnight.

About 45 minutes before you're ready to cook, prepare the coals for your grill in a chimney. Bring the chicken to room temperature as you wait on the coals. When the coals are hot and no longer flaming, pour them out of the chimney and into the grill; bank the coals to one side. Put the grate on, cover with the lid, and let it heat up for about 10 minutes. Give the grate a good scraping with a brush once hot. Soak a piece of paper towel with the oil and, using tongs, rub it on the grate to thoroughly coat.

Start cooking the chicken over the mostly gray coals, cooking skin side down for about 6 minutes. Put the lid on the grill to help prevent flare-ups. Flip the chicken pieces and move them to the cooler side of the grill and cook for 20 to 25 minutes, or until your instant-read thermometer reads at 165°F (75°C), flipping occasionally. Remove from the heat and let rest for 10 minutes, then season well with salt and serve the chicken pieces with lime wedges and charred onions.

super-rustic fish tacos with grilled pineapples, avocado, and salsa roja

Grapeseed or other neutral oil

1 medium-size ripe pineapple, cut in half lengthwise

3 whole white-fleshed fish, about 1 to 1.5 pounds (455 to 680 g) each (I like corvina, branzino, or trout; have the fishmonger gut and scale the fish for you)

Kosher salt

18 corn tortillas

1 sweet onion, thinly sliced

2 ripe medium avocados, cut into wedges

2 limes, cut into wedges

1 cup (240 ml) Smooth Smoked Chile Salsa Roja (page 343), to serve

Serves 6

Every afternoon on the beach at Punta Lobos near Todos Santos, local fishermen pull up in their Panga boats with the catch of the day, and you can choose from their silvery haul of yellowfin and corvina. Fish this good doesn't need much, but a chargrilled pineapple is a gorgeous accent.

Prepare a charcoal grill by heating until the flames die away and the coals are ashed over. Spread the coals, replace the grate, and wait for the grate to heat up, about 10 minutes. Give the grate a good scraping with a brush once hot. Soak a piece of paper towel with oil and, using tongs, rub it on the grate to thoroughly coat.

Rub the pineapple with oil on all sides and place it cut side down on the grill directly over the coals. Cook, without turning, until well charred, about 10 minutes, then flip and cook on the skin side for another 5 minutes. Remove from the grill and let rest for 5 minutes.

While the pineapple is cooking, rub the fish with oil and season with salt. Place on the grill and cook without turning for 4 to 5 minutes. Carefully flip each fish. Continue cooking until the fish is no longer transparent at the bone—one trick is to gently pull on the dorsal fin, and if it pulls out easily the fish is cooked.

Place the finished fish on a platter. Cut the top off the pineapple and cut the fruit into half-moons. Heat the tortillas on the grill, preferably atop a flat griddle or cast-iron pan to keep from scorching. Serve the fish with the pineapple, tortillas, onion, avocados, lime wedges, salsa, and extra salt and let everyone assemble their own tacos.

Fisherman Roman Orozco at Punta Lobos, Baja California Sur,
holding a Pacific jack

sustainability away from home

Dano's passion for the land and the sea of Baja Sur is infectious and deep-seated. The travel industry brings jobs but also disruption, and he wants to make sure development in his part of the beautiful coast is done responsibly. His own new home nearby is built with the low-impact rammed-earth method of construction, which keeps the house naturally cool even during the heat of a Baja summer.

While we were in Baja, Dano took us to visit his friend Jorge Guevara's farm, Baja Farm Fresh, located in Pescadero. The palm- and cactus-lined landscape is dotted with organic farms growing herbs and other crops for export. BFF is more focused on providing Baja Sur's culinary scene with gorgeous vegetables, both new world natives like squash and tomatoes and fennel and tatsoi greens and the prettiest little lettuces you've ever seen. Even early in the day, the heat in the field was intense, but the vegetables laid in neat sandy furrows seemed well watered. Dano pointed to the Sierra de la Luna mountain range just to our east and explained that Pescadero was right in the watershed of the high mountains, making irrigation feasible for the dry climate. All I know is that it was midwinter, and we had succulent cherry tomatoes and squash blossoms to play with in the kitchen!

It's easy, when you are traveling, to set aside normal concerns about sustainability, but I took inspiration from the commitment of Dano and his friends. He helped me find responsibly fished shrimp for my recipe testing. He helps connect chefs with quality organic produce. After seeing several bars and restaurants announce they didn't offer plastic straws, I was glad to learn that Baja Sur, the southern state of the Baja Peninsula, has been a leader in combating the plastic ocean waste that the area's tourism industry has exacerbated. A full ban on plastic bags, cups, and containers will go into effect there in 2021. It's a good reminder that we all share our oceans and that our travel can be taxing on oceanfront regions like Baja.

In addition to my political advocacy for ocean health at home, when I travel anywhere—Baja, Rome, or Normandy—I like to take a couple of very light shopping bags so I don't need plastic bags, and I have the Monterey Bay Aquarium's Seafood Watch app loaded on my phone to help me know if any unfamiliar fish (or unfamiliarly named fish) is a sustainable choice. These steps are not a replacement for visiting my legislators or raising money for ocean conservancies (see Resources, page 344), but they are reminders of our need for collective action.

Seattle

summery cocktails, dungeness crab, and potato chips

This book is all about travel, but there is nothing I love more than coming home after a trip. Sure, I might fantasize about living in that one château in Provence or eating Sicilian gelato every day of my life, but I love my Seattle home, where I live with Dan, my kitty, B, and my sad-eyed (but quite content) dog, Arlo. One of the greatest lessons travel can bring you is how to appreciate what home has in store for you.

My house has been the quiet complement to my bonkers restaurant life for eighteen years now—I bought it when I was young, single, and the brand-new owner of my first restaurant. I'm still startled by my youthful decisiveness in purchasing it, but it has evolved as I have. I've been making tweaks, small and large, ever since I moved in: hanging art,

planting trees, a big kitchen redo, and most recently a backyard refresh that included a woodburning oven built by Dan himself. It's great, and it even has a roof overhang so that we can cook in the inevitable rain.

The backyard has always been a favorite place to spend time with friends, but now we are out there all the time. We spread pretty vegetable, charcuterie, and cheese platters out on the marble table, fire up some pizzas, braises, or roasty vegetables, and spend long evenings nibbling, sipping, and occasionally getting another round of pies in the oven.

It's also a place where Dan and I take a pause, just the two of us, on the rare occasion where we both have an evening free. We will grab a snack—maybe chips with his delicious dill dip—and let the sun go down as we sip on spritzes (or if we are tired, a can of beer, the simplest spritz of all). Entertaining yourself and your dearest is just as important as putting on a thing for a crowd.

I might love being back home in Seattle, but my own tiny yard is a tribute to the things I've seen on the road. I'm working on a tidy cypress hedge to create the sense of structure, symmetry, and privacy that I love in French gardens. But I also cultivate the flowery excess of some English gardens: There are old-fashioned roses, of course, and in the late summer, my creamy-green hydrangeas are so heavy with blossoms they bend almost to the ground. I have an olive tree in a pot to remind me of my Mediterranean visits (though I haven't yet had a harvestable crop), and, of course, I have a kitchen garden, partially in containers and partially in the ground. Along with all the herbs, I have done pretty well growing hot-weather New World crops like tomatoes, cucumbers, and chiles. And in classic Seattle fashion, I've made room for dahlias in the garden. Though they originally came from Mexico, they are the official flower of Seattle, and they are shamelessly, delightfully showy. Mine are white pompoms with a sort of hallucinatory violet haze around the edge of each petal.

My backyard food has a freedom to blend customs and ideas with whatever is jumping out of the garden or market at any given time. I love to pack garden herbs into my cocktails, or grab a plum from my front-yard tree as the perfect accent to a quick-seared tuna loin. I'm always drawn to the casual way we have with seafood in the Northwest and try not to mess with that goodness too much, just adding an extra accent of foraged fennel or a prickle of good Calabrian chile paste to make it irresistible to dip some bread in the drippings. Anything to keep my people lingering around the table.

your favorite melon and mint mojitos

1 medium very ripe aromatic Charentais or cantaloupe melon, room temperature, peeled and cut into chunks (about 1 quart/1 L)

¼ cup (60 ml) Simple Syrup (more if your melon is not quite sweet enough; page 21)

Pinch of salt

½ cup (25 g) picked mint leaves, plus sprigs, to garnish

½ cup (115 ml) lime juice

12 ounces (340 ml) good-quality white rum, like Rhum JM

Soda water

Lime wedges, to garnish

Makes 6 cocktails

Out at the cabin, my mom had Tupperware for everything, including cantaloupe. She would keep a giant container filled with chilly sliced cantaloupe, all ready to go. We would pop the lid and get a big burst of melon aroma, and this cocktail works that summery smell into a clean, bright drink. One perfect melon supplies enough fragrance for a pitcher—not plastic, these days—of cooling drinks.

In a blender, combine the melon, simple syrup, and salt. Buzz until smooth, then chill in the fridge until very cold, roughly an hour.

Chill six cocktail glasses in the freezer. In a large glass pitcher, muddle the mint and lime juice. Pour in the rum, add some ice, and stir until very cold. Strain the rum and lime mixture into the glasses. Into each pour ½ cup (120 ml) melon puree. Top each glass with ice and a splash of soda. Give each drink a quick stir with a mint sprig. Garnish with the mint and a lime wedge.

pimm's cup with lemon verbena and mint

2 ounces (60 ml) Pimm's No. 1
¾ ounce (20 ml) lemon juice
(I like mine lemony!)
Fever-Tree ginger ale
Sliced strawberries, to garnish
Mint sprig, to garnish
Lemon verbena sprig, to
garnish

Makes 1 cocktail

I love the garnishes in a traditional Pimm's cup, made with the gin-based, iced tea–colored liquor called Pimm's No. 1. Too much Pimm's can be sweet, though—the key is to serve it very, very cold, and to use a hearty squeeze of lemon. I also like to boost the aroma with some lemon verbena, which grows a little too abundantly in my garden.

Fill a Collins glass with ice, then pour in the Pimm's, lemon juice, and the ginger ale. Give it a big stir, and then go crazy with your garnishes. I love strawberries, mint, and lemon verbena.

the way we were

¾ ounce (20 ml) Cap Corse
Quinquina Blanc
¾ ounce (20 ml) Lillet Rosé
½ ounce (15 ml) Cocchi Rosso
1 ounce (30 ml) soda water
3 ounces (90 ml) dry crémant
(such as Antech Crémant
de Limoux)
Large strip of grapefruit peel

Makes 1 cocktail

Brady Sprouse, who was our bar manager at Barnacle for three years, heard a rumor that I didn't like cocktails. It's not true (as the pages of this book devoted to cocktails attest)! I'm just choosy, that's all. I want a balanced, bracing cocktail that's not too strong, not too sweet, and full of complex flavors that remain just a little tricky to describe. So he set about to make one I would like, with a mix of light-handed bitters and bubbles to seal the deal. It's bright, summery pink, and refreshing, and he won me over, of course. I especially love it when I sip it through the grapefruit garnish.

In a stemmed glass three-quarters filled with ice, stir together the Cap Corse, Lillet Rosé, and Cocchi Rosso. Pour in the soda water and the sparkling wine and stir. Garnish with the grapefruit peel.

The Way We Were

white negroni

¾ ounce (20 ml) Suze
1½ ounces (40 ml) gin
1 ounce (30 ml) Lillet
Orange wedge, to garnish

Makes 1 cocktail

Suze is a funky, bitter aperitif: It's got a distinct earthiness that really rounds out a drink, with a touch of sweetness and citrus elements that soften it to keep it from feeling like homework. I like it mixed with the gentler Lillet in a riff on the negroni, and of course, that calls for a nice juicy orange wedge, as well.

Fill a rocks glass halfway with ice. In a cocktail shaker filled with ice, combine the Suze, gin, and Lillet. Shake until very cold and strain into the ready glass. Serve with a fat orange wedge.

strawberry and black pepper g&t

4 ounces (120 ml) gin
1 cup (200 g) strawberries (as ripe as they get)
Tonic water
Strawberries, to garnish
Black pepper, to garnish

Makes 2 cocktails

I don't remember the name of the London bar where I got inspired for this drink, but I'm sure I wasn't the one who ordered their strawberry and pepper drink. It sounded too odd: strawberry-muddled white wine, maybe even muscadet, with ground black pepper all over it. I tasted it, though, and I loved the strawberries with the pungent pepper. I can't imagine muddling muscadet at home, and I liked the combo even better with a brisk G&T. Perfect for the strawberry explosion that happens all over my front yard every June.

In a cocktail shaker, muddle the strawberries with the gin. Strain into an empty glass.

Fill two highball glasses with ice and strain the strawberry gin a second time, dividing it between the two glasses. Top each glass with tonic and garnish with a few strawberries, both in the gin and hanging from the side. Grind two or three twists of black pepper over the top of each drink.

Strawberry and Black Pepper G&T

garden to glass

The Columbia River Gorge region makes for spectacular driving, meandering past rolling hills through vineyards and farms, and always coming back, once again, to views of the majestic Columbia River. The region includes both Washington and Oregon, and it is tremendously varied terrain; that variation is one of the reasons it's a favorite Northwest winemaking region for me, with established wineries like Syncline and Analemma and promising young wineries like the Color Collector. Though the landscape provides many varieties of viticulture, in general the wine here nods to the lower alcohol, higher elevation European wines I love so much.

To visit the gorge is to dig into a different kind of Northwest beauty than I experience at home in Seattle. One of my favorite spots is Hiyu Wine Farm, founded by Nate Ready and China Tresemer, a biodiverse diverse farm and vineyard with a real commitment to integrative agriculture. The vines grow in untilled soil and share their space with beneficial plants. The farm's pigs, cows, chicken, ducks, and geese help with vegetation control. Tastings have a similarly holistic feel: In the "wine tavern," you don't sip wine unaccompanied—instead, the wines are presented alongside beautiful small plates of food that entwine with the flavor of the wines, including a robust, almost light-red rosé and a startlingly rich and minerally albariño. I had the pleasure of cooking a special dinner at Hiyu with my friend, their executive chef, Jason Barwikowski, and it was so easy to be inspired by the grazing livestock, the lush plantings, the view of Mount Hood, and of course, the good wine, which had both wildness and refinement bursting forth.

I don't have a wholly integrated farm to work with back in Seattle, but I do like to bring a little bit of unruly vegetation into my drinking. Sometimes that might just mean drinking rosé or a delicious beer from my favorite neighborhood brewery, Holy Mountain, in the backyard. Speaking of beer: Right in our metaphorical backyard, in Washington's Yakima Valley a couple of hours away, 75 percent of US hops crops are grown.

Summer also encourages me to work the local lushness into cocktails. Once summer starts jumping, I always have more herbs than I can handle in the garden. It's not really a problem, since I can always figure out a way to use them: in after-dinner infusions (fresh mint plus hot water = tea!), in floral arrangements, and—even more fun—in cocktails.

I'll muddle not just mint, but basil, lemon verbena, or cilantro into my juleps and mojitos. Shaking a sprig of a heartier herb like sage, thyme, or rosemary into a cocktail can also be really interesting—they have a more savory quality than tender herbs. Take Cocchi Bianco, shaken with some rosemary—ooh that's good, especially with an orange twist.

It's also easy to infuse herbs into a simple syrup (see page 21). Try throwing a few sprigs of tarragon or cilantro into the hot syrup, let it cool, and then strain before swirling into a drink. A sage syrup is surprisingly delicious stirred into a gin and tonic.

Infusions are less spontaneous, but they look so pretty on a liquor shelf—like the vivid green of bay leaves as they soak in a bottle of vodka. And, of course, herbs, particularly herb flowers, make the prettiest garnishes for summer cocktails. A vivid yellow cucumber flower or a violet-blue stem of blossoming borage bring the garden to the glass. Whether it's wine or cocktails, the Pacific Northwest way is to rejoice in the abundant, slightly unruly growth of our region.

summer tartine with ricotta and figs

Every year around my early August birthday, I go with one of my chefs, Taylor Thornhill, to pick figs from the tree at the school where my brother works. These are early-ripening green figs that are as big as lemons and much heavier. When you cut into them, their interiors are magenta red, jammy, and absurdly juicy. They don't need much to go with them, but a sturdy raft of grilled bread keeps the figs from bursting in your hands, and fresh ricotta gives them some gentle, creamy contrast. Go a little nuts with the black pepper on this tartine—it's a beautiful match with the figs.

4 (¾-inch/2-cm) slices good sourdough bread, grilled and cooled to room temperature (see page 20 for some tips on grilling bread)

Salt

1 cup (240 ml) good whole-milk ricotta (on the West Coast look for Bellwether)

1 pint (500 g) ripe figs, stemmed, then halved or quartered

Olive oil, to garnish

Crunchy sea salt and freshly ground black pepper, to finish

Serves 4 to 6

Season the grilled bread with a bit of salt. Generously spread each slice with ricotta. You can serve each guest a big tartine, or cut each slice into 2 or 3 pieces for hand-held eating.

Place the ricotta toast on a serving plate and top with a few pieces of the figs. Drizzle with olive oil and generously season with crunchy salt and pepper.

chilled marinated mussels with pickled celery and tarragon

1 tablespoon olive oil

1 large shallot, sliced into ¼-inch (6-mm) rounds

2 pounds (910 g) mussels, scrubbed, debearded, and thoroughly checked for cracks (see headnote, page 147)

2 cups (480 ml) white wine

½ teaspoon salt, plus more to taste

¼ cup (60 ml) white wine vinegar, plus more to taste

1 cup (240 ml) very good extra-virgin olive oil—use your special bottle for this!

1 cup (340 g) Pickled Celery, sliced ¼ inch (6 mm) thick on the bias (page 340)

1 cup (225 g) cherry tomatoes, quartered

¼ cup (13 g) tarragon leaves

Buttery crackers or sliced baguette, to serve

Lemon Aioli (page 338) or mayonnaise (I like Best Foods/Hellmann's; optional)

Serves 6 to 8

Cold mussels may be even better than warm ones, one reason I have a couple of recipes for them in this book. While the mint-pistou ones on page 147 are rich, these are very lightly pickled, brisk, and fragrant with tarragon—one of mussels' best companions. The other great thing is that this recipe is best made ahead of time to develop flavors well, and it will hold for two to three days in the fridge. That way, you can be as cool and collected as a chilled mussel when your guests arrive.

In a large pan or Dutch oven over medium-high, heat the 1 tablespoon olive oil. Add the shallot and cook for about 3 minutes. Add the mussels, wine, and salt. Cover and steam the mussels for 3 to 4 minutes, until they have all opened. You can pull out the cooked ones into a separate bowl, then cover the pot to allow the slow ones to cook a bit more. Toss out any mussels that don't open after 3 to 4 more minutes. Transfer the rest of the mussels to the bowl and chill in the refrigerator until they are cool enough to handle. When cool, pull each mussel out of its shell and pull off any stray beards. Place the cleaned mussels in a medium bowl along with any shallot rings that are easy to pick out. Pour the vinegar and good olive oil over the mussels. Add the pickled celery and toss well. Refrigerate overnight.

Fifteen minutes before serving, pull the mussels from the fridge to let the olive oil soften. Toss the mussel mixture well and taste a mussel; adjust the seasoning with a little salt or vinegar, if desired. Fold in the cherry tomatoes and the tarragon. Serve with buttery crackers; these make lovely little canapés with a swash of aioli on a cracker.

dill dip with potato chips

1 cup (240 ml) European-style whole-milk yogurt, such as Straus
1 cup (240 ml) sour cream
1 small garlic clove, grated
2 tablespoons olive oil, plus more to garnish
1 tablespoon lemon juice
Salt and freshly ground black pepper
½ cup (25 g) fresh dill fronds, minced, plus a few whole fronds or flowers, to garnish
Potato chips (see page 304 to make your own, or pick a favorite brand), to serve

Serves 6 to 8

Dips are the best, and not just because I like any occasion to serve potato chips. Dips are just so easy to eat, and you can focus on one big flavor: Here, it's a garden's worth of dill. You can mix the body of the dip a day in advance, but make sure the dill is freshly chopped and swirled in at the last minute. You need it to be boldly fragrant. If you want to make the dish a little fancier, go nuts and spoon some salmon caviar on top.

In a medium bowl, combine the yogurt, sour cream, garlic, olive oil, lemon juice, and salt and pepper. Just before serving, fold in the dill. Place in a serving dish and garnish with olive oil and more dill or dill flowers. This dip will taste best the day it is made.

salt and pepper potato chips

1 cup (240 ml) distilled vinegar
6 russet potatoes, skin on
About 8 cups (1.9 L) neutral
oil, such as canola or
grapeseed oil, for frying
Salt and freshly ground black
pepper

Serves 8 to 10

We considered calling this book "All About Chips" or "Renee Loves Chips." I eat them everywhere I travel, from Nashville to Normandy. Every now and then it's fun to make them at home. They are surprisingly simple to make—as long as you don't crowd that pan!—and frying them is a great little bit of theater for a gathering. Fresh fried food makes everyone absurdly excited, and for good reason. As much as I love a good bag of chips, a slightly warm chip is just dreamy. In this recipe, we add vinegar to the soaking water for salt 'n' vinegar flavor and to prevent the potato slices from browning. Serve with a favorite dip or just with a glass of sparkling wine!

In a large bowl, whisk together 8 cups (1.9 L) water and the vinegar.

Using a mandolin, slice the potatoes as thinly as possible, placing the slices in the vinegar water as you work. After a while, the screw can loosen on the mandolin, so make sure to keep adjusting the blade to keep the slices translucent. Discard the ends of the potatoes (or save them for another use).

Drain the potatoes. Place a layer of paper towels on a baking sheet and lay a single layer of potato slices across it. Place another paper towel layer on top and repeat for about half the potato slices. Use a second baking sheet to layer the second half of the slices with paper towels.

When ready to cook, have ready a spider or a slotted spoon and a wire cooling rack set atop a baking sheet. In a heavy 4-quart (4.5-liter) saucepan or Dutch oven, heat 2 to 3 inches (5 to 7.5 cm) oil to 350°F (175°C). Carefully drop in a generous handful of potato slices, stirring to separate them. Fry, stirring occasionally, until the potatoes are light golden brown, about 5 minutes. Remember, this is a long percolating process, not a sudden one. Remove the chips to the prepared rack and season with salt and pepper right away.

Make sure the oil temperature comes back to 350°F (175°C), adjusting heat if necessary, before repeating with the next batch. Continue until all the potatoes are fried. These taste best the day they are cooked.

clam dip with saltines
(or potato chips, of course)

Hey, here's one more way to savor good canned seafood, like the beautiful Galician cockles that Matiz imports from Spain—mix it into a good ol' 1950s-style dip. I'm not sure your grandmother would have added a shower of finely grated lemon zest to make it fragrant and bright, but I think it's a good, modern touch.

In a medium bowl, beat the cream cheese with a sturdy whisk until it is soft and fluffy. Whisk in the sour cream and mix well. Stir in the lemon zest, lemon juice, black pepper, and hot sauce. Fold in the clams. Check the texture and use some clam juice to thin it to a nice dipping consistency, if necessary. Mix in three-quarters of the chives. Taste and add salt if necessary, then refrigerate until ready to serve. The dip can be made a day in advance but wait to add the chives until the last minute.

The dip will firm up a bit in the fridge. Garnish with the rest of the minced chives and serve with saltines.

8 ounces (225 g) cream cheese, at room temperature

1½ cups (350 g) sour cream

Zest of 1 lemon

4 teaspoons lemon juice

Freshly ground black pepper

1 tablespoon hot sauce, such as Tapatío

2 (4-ounce/120-g) cans Matiz canned clams, drained with the liquid reserved, gently chopped

¼ cup (11 g) minced chives

Salt (optional)

Saltines or potato chips (see page 304 to make your own, or pick a favorite brand), to serve

Serves 8 to 10

Grilled coho salmon at Spee-Bi-Dah, Washington

dates and manchego

2 tablespoons olive oil, plus a
    bit more to drizzle
12 ounces (340 g) Medjool
    dates
Crunchy sea salt, to finish
6 ounces (170 g) crumbled
    Manchego cheese

Serves 6 to 8

Sometimes it takes just a little heat to transform an ingredient, like dates, which go from being stiff and fudgy to luscious and aromatic with a little gentle heating. Salty sheep's milk Manchego is the perfect counterpart.

Pour the olive oil into a large, heavy skillet and place over medium heat. Add the dates, watch carefully, and turn each date after it has plumped and turned a bit rusty in color, about 90 seconds. Cook the second side of each date, about 45 seconds. Turn the pan off, and remove the dates from the pan. Watch out: All that sugar makes them burn easily.

Place the dates on a serving plate in a pretty pile. Sprinkle with crunchy salt and then sprinkle the Manchego on top. Drizzle the plate with additional olive oil and serve with toothpicks.

zucchini fritters

It's a cliché, but you must get creative if you have a zucchini vine in your garden because you will be drowning in them by about mid-August. It's a wonderful problem to have. So along with grilling and shredding them into zucchini bread, frying is a delightful way to transform zucchini. Here, the shredded zucchini is intertwined with so many garden herbs; I gave you a guideline, but really most herbs will taste great here—whatever your garden is overproducing along with the zucchini.

Coarsely grate the zucchini and the potato and toss with 2 teaspoons salt in a large bowl. Transfer to a colander and let drain for at least 1 hour. Grab handfuls of the zucchini mixture and squeeze, squeeze, squeeze to extract the extra moisture from the vegetables. Discard the liquid.

In a large bowl, stir together the zucchini mixture, eggs, half the grated garlic, the flour, parsley, marjoram, chives, mint, fennel, and black pepper.

Have ready a slotted spoon or a spider and a sheet pan lined with either a wire cooling rack or a double layer of paper towels, which you will need to change frequently. In a large iron skillet over medium-high, heat the ¼ cup (60 ml) of olive oil and canola oil together until the oil bubbles vigorously when a drop of the batter is placed in it; don't let it heat so much that it smokes.

Use a spoon to ease ¼ cup (30 g) of the zucchini mixture at a time into the hot oil; drop about three dollops at a time. Cook undisturbed for about 1 to 1½ minutes until browned, then carefully flip each fritter. Cook until browned on the other side, another 1 to 1½ minutes. Remove to the rack and season with salt. Repeat the process with the remaining zucchini mixture.

In a medium bowl, whisk together the yogurt, the remaining garlic, 2 tablespoons olive oil, and the lemon juice.

Arrange the fritters on a plate and decorate with some of the yogurt mixture. Sprinkle the parsley and chives on top. Season with the crunchy salt and serve.

3 pounds (1.4 kg) zucchini (about 3 large)
1 russet potato, peeled
2 teaspoons salt, plus more for seasoning
2 large eggs, lightly beaten
2 garlic cloves, grated
⅓ cup (40 g) all-purpose flour
2 tablespoons minced Italian parsley leaves
1 tablespoon minced fresh marjoram leaves
1 tablespoon minced chives
2 tablespoons minced fresh mint leaves
1 teaspoon toasted ground fennel seeds
Freshly ground black pepper
¼ cup (60 ml) olive oil (and more if needed), plus 2 tablespoons
¼ cup (60 ml) canola or other neutral oil (and more if needed)
1 cup (240 ml) European-style yogurt, such as Straus—if you only have Greek, whisk in some water or olive oil to make it drizzle-able
1 tablespoon freshly squeezed lemon juice
2 tablespoons whole parsley leaves, plus a few flowers, if available
2 tablespoons chives, cut into 1-inch (2.5-cm) sticks, plus a few flowers, if available
Crunchy sea salt

Serves 8 to 10

rockfish crudo with ajo blanco and roasted serrano oil

4 ounces (115 g) blanched
   almonds
2 ounces (60 g) stale bread,
   trimmed of crust
2 small garlic cloves, peeled
9 tablespoons (130 ml) olive oil
1 tablespoon sherry vinegar
1 teaspoon salt, plus more to
   taste
1½ teaspoons freshly squeezed
   lemon juice
1 pound (455 g) rockfish fillets,
   bones and skins removed,
   cut into ½-inch (12-mm)
   chunks
Zest of 1 lime
1 tablespoon lime juice, plus
   more to taste
½ cup (120 ml) Roasted
   Serrano Oil (page 342)
1 serrano pepper, thinly sliced
Calendula petals (optional)

Serves 4 to 6

Though this is a dish I created with Seattle in mind, it was inspired by running into a Seattle connection in Paris. Rob Mendoza, who worked at Lummi Island's The Willows Inn before moving to France, is the chef at a chic wine bar and restaurant, Le Saint Sébastien, where he combines classic flavors with lightness and sweet romanticism. When we ate there, I was wild about his perfectly fried sardines, which were served in a pretty puddle of *ajo blanco*, the cold soup made with bread, almonds, and garlic. The idea of that toasty-flavored chilled soup with seafood stuck with me. I layered mine with cool cubes of raw fish and the roasted serrano oil.

Heat the oven to 325°F (170°C).

Place the almonds on a baking sheet and toast until just beginning to color, about 8 minutes. Let them cool to room temperature.

Soak the bread in 1 cup (240 ml) water for 10 minutes.

Place all but a dozen almonds in a blender and pulse to chop coarsely. Add the bread and soaking water, the garlic, 7 table-spoons (100 ml) of the olive oil, the vinegar, salt, and lemon juice. Buzz at high speed until the ajo blanco is smooth.

In a medium bowl, toss the rockfish with the lime zest, lime juice, 2 tablespoons olive oil, and salt.

On a deep, chilled platter, spoon in the ajo blanco, then top with the rockfish mixture. Spoon on some serrano oil, using a light drizzle for a mild taste or a bolder hand for more spice. Taste the rockfish and adjust the seasoning with more salt and lime juice.

Crush the remaining almonds with a mortar and pestle (or roughly chop them) and sprinkle them atop the rockfish along with the serrano slices and calendula petals if you have some in your garden. Sprinkle with additional salt and lime and eat right away.

grilled oysters with fermented chile butter

1 cup (2 sticks/225 g) unsalted butter, softened

1½ cups (360 ml) Fermented Hot Sauce (page 337)

2 dozen fresh 3-inch (7.5-cm) oysters, shucked, on the half shell

1 lime, halved

Serves 4 to 6

Grilling is the classic Pacific Northwest way to eat oysters—it's also great for larger oysters or summertime oysters, when they may be spawning and less bright and savory for raw eating. Cooking firms them up and evens out the flavors. My tips for a grilled oyster? Shuck them first—that way you can maintain all the butter in the shell. Also, make sure the butter baste has plenty of flavor, like this chile butter made with homemade hot sauce. This is a great first fermentation project—it doesn't take long, nor is it to space-consuming, and it's so lively and satisfying. Cold beer is a must, of course.

In a stand mixer fitted with the paddle attachment, beat the butter on medium for about 2 minutes, until it increases in volume and starts to lighten in color. Turn the mixer to low and carefully pour in the hot sauce, adjusting the amount of hot sauce to your preferred spiciness level. I like 1½ cups (360 ml), which is pretty spicy but not painful. You can roll the spicy butter into logs and freeze it for up to a month to later put on grilled steaks or roasted chicken.

Light a charcoal fire in a grill, and when the coals are ashed over, spread them out evenly and replace the grate. Have a serving platter covered in rock salt ready.

Spoon a teaspoon of butter onto each oyster and place it on the hot grate. Cook uncovered for 3 minutes. Cover the grill and cook for 3 minutes, or until the butter around the edges is actively bubbling and the oysters are nicely firm. Making sure not to tip the juices into the hot coals, place the oysters on the prepared platter. Squeeze with lime juice and serve right away.

tomato tonnato

Beige as beige can be, *tonnato* sauce might be a little bit dowdy to look at, but I've loved it for a long time. It's full of complex, long-playing flavors and is super simple to make. When I was last in London, we had a spectacular dish of tomatoes with tonnato at Luca, a favorite Italian-style restaurant of mine. I loved the look of the showy red tomatoes playing peekaboo with the plain sauce. The sharp little garnishes help balance it all out.

In a blender, combine the tuna, anchovies, garlic, and capers and buzz into a coarse paste. Add the olive oil, mayonnaise, and lemon juice and blend until smooth. Taste and season with salt and pepper. The sauce can be made and stored in the refrigerator up to a day ahead.

Arrange the tomatoes on a serving platter and season with crunchy salt. Cover with the tuna mayonnaise. Garnish with the pickled celery, caperberries, and black pepper; serve right away.

1 (6-ounce/170-g) can water-packed, line-caught West Coast albacore tuna (I like St. Jude)

4 anchovy fillets

2 garlic cloves, smashed

2 tablespoons capers, preferably salted, rinsed, soaked, and drained

½ cup (120 ml) olive oil

¾ cup (180 ml) mayonnaise (I like Best Foods/Hellmann's)

¼ cup (60 ml) lemon juice

Salt and freshly ground black pepper

3 large ripe beefsteak or heirloom tomatoes, sliced into thick slices

Crunchy sea salt, to finish

About 2 tablespoons Pickled Celery (page 340), drained

2 tablespoons sliced caperberries, or capers

Serves 6 to 8

tinned fish spectacular

One of my favorite places to browse in Seattle, or honestly in the world, is DeLaurenti, the specialty foods store in the heart of Pike Place Market. It is filled with the loveliest fancy foods from the States and around the world. First, I will stop by the cheese counter for a few samples from their encyclopedic collection. Then I'll look through their olive oils, vinegars, beautiful pastas, and esoteric jams. I always save the canned seafood selection for last because I find myself loading up my basket in the face of so many beautifully packaged, slightly mysterious tins. Of course, sardines are old friends, but one time I might give cockles a try, or another day I'll really go for it with a big tin of sprats.

I love having the seafood in my cupboards, in no small part because its tins and boxes are so striking graphically: In Europe, canneries compete for the most jewel-like packaging. People pick up tinned fish as a special postcard from seaside tourist towns and give them as pretty little gifts. While European canneries treat their seafood beautifully in terms of preserving, they are also willing to can some fish I make sure to avoid, due to overfishing. If I am buying an unfamiliar fish, I check out its profile on Monterey Bay Seafood Watch to make sure I'm not accidentally buying bluefin tuna or beluga whale or something.

Besides looking pretty in their packaging, tinned fish also make for a great unplanned party. I'll pull several cans out of my shelves, open them up, and plunk them on a table with a baguette, some buttery crackers, lemon wedges, soft butter, and mustard. Oh, and you know me by now, I'll have something pickle-y too, like tart green piparra peppers (also from DeLaurenti).

Each tin of seafood is a fun little mystery box to discover. With a little crowd around you, you can nibble here and there and argue over favorites. It's a surprisingly satisfying quasi-meal, and you'll eat more seafood than you might expect.

Sprats are tiny and beautifully laid out in their can. Mackerel, which has a reputation for being strong-flavored, is actually quite fresh and mild. Sardines and anchovies are stronger, which is why they taste so delicious on bread, with butter and some chile paste spooned on. Octopus is just delicious canned, and so much easier to prepare that way. In general, I opt for unseasoned tinned fish, though I do sometimes enjoy the seasoned varieties, like anchovies preserved with Calabrian chiles. It's always worth a try. José Gourmet, Matiz, and Ortiz are some favorite brands to look for, and Patagonia has recently launched a really tasty line of preserved (and sustainably farmed) seafood whose mussels I particularly like.

Of course, wine is delightful alongside your seafood spread, and you'll need something to cut some of the richness on the table. Dry rosé, like Syncline's crisp blend, is a natural choice. You could also look for the more esoteric white Cabernet Franc from Jackalope Wine Cellars on the Oregon side of the Columbia Gorge—it's peppery and herbaceous but sunny and light, too—a great foil for the rich fish.

chanterelles, soft scrambled eggs, and seaweed butter

4 tablespoons (60 ml) olive oil

8 ounces (225 g) chanterelles, trimmed, brushed clean, and halved or quartered if very large

¼ cup (115 g) Seaweed Butter (page 342)

6 large eggs

Salt and freshly ground black pepper

Toast or grilled bread, to serve (see page 20 for tips on grilling bread)

Serves 2 to 4

Golden chanterelles have a somewhat apricot aroma and appear in Seattle markets in midsummer, sweet and small, as shown here, but as fall begins, they become larger and more abundant. The price plummets, and I can really pile them up in my cooking. They are so good with a dollop of Seaweed Butter (page 342), combined with a golden soft heap of scrambled eggs.

My method of soft scrambled eggs is exactly the opposite of what most people will say to do. I like to use my very well-seasoned steel skillet and work with high heat and constant folding to make soft, high ridges in the eggs. The whole thing comes together very quickly. Like, make sure you have your serving plate next to the stove before you start, because if you turn around from the pan, you'll likely end up with rubbery eggs.

In a wide heavy skillet over medium, heat 2 tablespoons of the olive oil. Add the chanterelles and sauté for about 8 minutes, stirring often. Add the seaweed butter and sauté the mushrooms for another minute, then set aside.

In a medium bowl, mix the eggs with a fork until blended but not completely homogenous or aerated. Season with salt.

Have a serving plate ready near the stove. Heat a very well-seasoned steel skillet on high and add the remaining 2 tablespoons olive oil. When the oil starts to glisten, pour in the eggs. With a rubber spatula, move the eggs around, scraping the bottom slowly and making sheets of soft eggs. After 30 seconds, reduce the heat to medium; keep cooking and turning the eggs. Never stop folding. Once the eggs are mostly firm but still wet, remove them from the pan to the serving plate. (Don't leave them in the pan, or they will continue to cook in the residual heat.) The total cooking time might be 1 minute—so fast!

Season with more salt, if desired, and black pepper. Spoon the chanterelles over the eggs and serve immediately with toast or grilled bread.

grilled and raw tomatoes with cucumbers, yogurt, and all the herbs

5 tablespoons (75 ml) olive oil,
   plus more to garnish
2 large beefsteak tomatoes,
   cored and quartered
Salt
2 English cucumbers, or
   4 smaller cucumbers,
   peeled, seeded, and cut
   into ¾-inch (2-cm) chunks
1 large red onion, cut into
   ¼-inch (6-mm) slices
1 pint (275 g) cherry tomatoes,
   halved
Juice of 1 lime
1 cup (50 g) dill fronds
1 cup (50 g) mint leaves
1 bunch well-washed cilantro,
   stems included, chopped
1 cup (240 ml) whole-milk
   yogurt, not Greek-style
   (I like Straus)
2 tablespoons Aleppo pepper
Crunchy sea salt, to finish

Serves 6 to 8

I know there are a lot of tomato recipes in this section, but this is the truth about how I eat. When it's summer and I can get great, locally grown tomatoes (sometimes from my own backyard!) I eat them all the time, and in great quantity. In November, after I have pickled my last green tomato, that's it. I don't really eat any fresh tomatoes until the next summer. Of course I'll use plenty of canned, dried, and even the occasional frozen tomato in my cooking.

So while the getting is good and there are too many tomatoes in every shape and color, I'll make a salad like this that plays with different textures and levels of juiciness. I grill a few big beefsteaks to a charry succulence and lay them as a foundation for pretty, fresh cherry tomatoes and cucumbers. The cooked tomato juices swirl with a tart vinaigrette and creamy yogurt, and piles of herbs freshen everything up. It's all just the right kind of too much.

Heat a large cast-iron skillet over medium-high heat. Pour in about 1 tablespoon olive oil and swirl around. Add the beefsteak tomatoes, season with salt, and sear, leaving them until they begin to brown and caramelize. Place the roasted tomatoes on a serving platter.

In a large bowl, toss together the cucumbers, onion, and cherry tomatoes. Toss with 4 tablespoons (60 ml) of the olive oil and the lime juice. Season with salt. Add about half the dill, mint, and cilantro, folding gently. Place the cucumber mixture atop the seared tomatoes on the platter. Top with the remaining herbs. Spoon the yogurt on top of the salad and sprinkle with the Aleppo pepper and crunchy salt. Drizzle the salad with olive oil to create pretty golden rivulets in the yogurt. Serve right away.

Mom and Dad, digging clams at Spee-Bi-Dah, Washington

pacific northwest foraging

Someone stole my plums. I was waiting eagerly for my Santa Rosa plum tree to ripen, and just before I was ready to gather them, some thief came and stripped the tree bare. Raccoons and squirrels can be a bother in my neighborhood, but the sheer thoroughness of the theft left no question that the perp was human.

I am still pissed off, but there is part of me that recognizes the thief's compulsion. Seattle is a city where food just kind of offers itself up everywhere. Walking down the sidewalk, you're likely to squash your flip-flop into a juicy little cherry that's dropped from a branch high above or spot several squirrel-nibbled apples on the median. Figs ripen on street corners, wild fennel crops up in empty lots, and well, the blackberries, they grow in every half-neglected yard, highway overpass, park boundary, and hillside in the city. I can't tell you how many times I have come across someone at the side of the road plucking and eating blackberries in a late-summer stupor.

That's before you even leave the city! So many of my best memories come from finding unexpected food—to call it foraging implies a little more planning than I usually give it. There are the varnish clams that have taken over the beach near my parents' cabin—invasive but delicious, and very easy to dig up. There are the morels I've found spontaneously in campgrounds and the golden trails of chanterelles I've followed while walking a logging road near Hama Hama, my favorite oyster farm on the Hood Canal.

You know you are truly home when you know what's edible everywhere you go, and Washington is especially lush. So I suppose I understand the impulse to pluck when you discover a tempting tree, limbs groaning with heavy fruit. But before you start harvesting, ask the occupant of the house. Seriously. It could be my tree. And I might be waiting for my plums to ripen perfectly.

pan-seared albacore with plums, melon, tahini, and pickled chiles

12 ounces (340 g) fresh albacore tuna loin, trimmed of any silver skin or blemishes

2 tablespoons olive oil

Salt and freshly ground black pepper

¼ cup (60 ml) tahini (I like Villa Jerada brand)

¼ cup (60 ml) whole-milk yogurt, such as Straus

1 small Charentais-style melon, seeded, thinly sliced, and cut into bite-size pieces

1 perfect plum, sliced in thin half moons

1 batch Pickled Fresno Chiles (page 340)

Really good olive oil, to finish

Lime wedges, for juice and to serve

Crunchy sea salt, to finish

Serves 4 to 6

At the Walrus and the Carpenter, we don't just serve oysters raw; we also love raw clams, scallops, and fin fish, too. Line-caught albacore is a favorite in season, and its accompaniments are ever-evolving, depending on what is glorious at the market at a given moment. This dish, with barely seared tuna, couldn't be more late-summer if it tried, with plums, melons, and sharp little rings of pickled chiles. The tahini keeps it all earthy and grounded. When you make a plate like this, make sure the grace notes don't overwhelm the tuna. You want to see plenty of tuna peeking out amid the beautiful fruit.

Rub the tuna with 1 tablespoon of the olive oil and season with salt and pepper.

Heat a cast-iron pan over medium-high heat. Pour 1 tablespoon oil into the pan, heat for 30 seconds, then set the tuna in it. Sear the tuna about 1½ minutes per side on each side, aiming for a golden-brown crust and a rare center. Remove the tuna from the pan and let it cool.

Slice the cooled tuna into ½-inch (12-mm) slices. Whisk the tahini with the yogurt until smooth and spoon it onto a serving platter. Season with salt. Arrange the tuna slices atop the tahini mixture, then top with pieces of the melon, plum, and wheels of pickled chile, making sure that you can see part of each slice of tuna. Drizzle generously with fancy olive oil, squeeze over some lime juice, and spoon around some pickled fresno juice. Sprinkle with crunchy salt and serve with lime wedges.

how to cook and clean a dungeness crab

Tell me what crab you eat, and I can tell you where you are from. In my world, there is really only one crab: Dungeness, with its orange shell after cooking and its mild, succulent meat. If you want to try other crab in this recipe, I'm sure the fennel butter will taste great with it, but I don't spend time cooking other crab. It's Dungeness or bust in my kitchen.

I've got to be honest with you, I've recently changed my tune on how to cook live crab. And my new method is intense, but it's so good. If you don't have the heart for it, by all means stick with my old standard of plunging one or two crabs into a pot of boiling water for 8 minutes (7 if you are planning to make the grilled crab on page 331) and then icing them off to stop the cooking.

But, if you are feeling brave, and you want crab that is meatier and less watery, then try this: First, chill the crabs by placing them on a bed of ice and covering them with ample ice for 15 minutes or so; this will make them sluggish. Meanwhile, assemble a large steamer (like your pasta pot, with a steamer insert set inside). Fill with water to just below the bottom of the insert and bring that to a rolling boil. Cover the pot with a snug lid. You can keep it on simmer while you prep the crabs and then get it rolling again.

Now for the hard part. Get a screwdriver, or something similarly hard and pointy. Turn a live crab on its back and position the screwdriver right above the center of the segmented tail flap at the bottom of the belly. Stab the crab, quickly. You will kill it immediately.

Now, stick your finger or a butter knife under that segmented tail flap and use that leverage to crack the back shell of the crab off. Remove the feathery gills and scoop out the guts inside the body of the crab.

Break the legs off the crab, making sure to include the meaty bits where the legs meet the crab body. I like to hold both sides of the crab legs and fold the crab in on itself. There is a seam in the middle of the body where it will naturally break. Make extra sure all the guts are removed (even the light yellow stuff). It will turn black and taint the meat if you leave it there. Keep the legs on ice while you process any other crabs.

Get the steamer fully boiling again, place the legs in the steamer, cover snugly, and steam for 8 minutes. Cool the legs immediately by placing them on a tray and right into the fridge.

We have a house rule that if it's a crab feast, you crack your own. But if you are preparing a dish with crabmeat (like crab melts or crab salad), here's how: Use hands to pull meat from the place where the legs meet the body, being careful to pry away all of the bits of papery shell (they look a lot like crabmeat). Use a cracker to gently crack the thicker leg shell and remove the meat by hand. Keep the crabmeat cold, cold, cold before serving.

grilled dungeness crab
with fennel butter

My dad, Jim Erickson, is a major reason I see food as an adventure. He loves harvesting food from the wild. Especially crabs! I grew up eating crab we caught all together in the Salish Sea. A lot of crab. So much that I remember getting a little tired of eating crab: crab toast, crab omelet, crab quiche, cold crab, and mostly crab melts. These days, I don't get to go crabbing as often, and so I'm completely ready to dig into a crab any time I have the chance. I especially love the smoky fragrance that comes when buttered crab hits a hot grill. I like to garnish it with big fennel blossoms that bloom all over Seattle roadsides and parking lots in the middle of the summer—lovely blooms and extra fennel fragrance all at once. (If you are really industrious, you can dry your own fennel blossoms and sift out their pollen so you don't have to splurge on the Italian stuff. But for mere mortals, order some from World Spice or Zingerman's, and know that you will have profound flavoring power in that spendy little jar.)

12 ounces (340 g) unsalted butter, softened
4 teaspoons fennel pollen
1 teaspoon salt
2 tablespoons lemon juice
2 whole cooked Dungeness crabs, gills, carapace, and brown bits removed, quartered (for tips on cooking and cleaning Dungeness crabs, see page 329)
Lemon juice, to garnish
Crusty bread, to serve

Serves 4 to 6 as an appetizer, 2 as a main course

In a stand mixer fitted with the paddle attachment, beat the butter, fennel pollen, salt, and lemon juice until fluffy and silky. Set aside.

Crack the claws and big joints of the crab. Brush the crab all over with butter, patting it on any exposed flesh particularly.

Prepare a charcoal grill by heating until the flames die away and the coals are ashed over. (Since the crab is so buttery, you will have an inferno if you rush this process.) Spread the coals, replace the grate, and wait for the grate to heat up, about 10 minutes.

Place the buttered crab on the grate and cover the grill. Cook for 3½ minutes, then remove the crab pieces to a serving platter, making sure not to tip the juices from the belly sections into the fire. Spoon any remaining butter over the hot crab. Serve with lemon and bread.

grilled wild coho salmon steaks with hazelnut tarator

2 tablespoons olive oil, plus a bit extra for the grate

6 wild-caught coho or sockeye salmon steaks, cut about 1¾ to 2 inches (4 to 5 cm) thick (if you have a whole fish, include the collar as well—it's delicious)

2 lemons, halved crosswise

Kosher salt and freshly ground black pepper

1 batch Hazelnut Tarator (page 337)

24 Pickled Sweet 100 Cherry Tomatoes (page 341)

Serves 6 to 8

I wrote earlier about how much I like to cook and eat meat on the bone. I've decided it's time to bring back the salmon steak, which lost popularity to the easier-to-gobble salmon fillet. For grilling, steaks are magic. They are easy to cook, less likely to fall apart, and the bones and connective tissue make for a richer flavor. Even better, everyone can roll up their sleeves and have fun with the process of pulling the salmon apart and eating it. It's like a salmon scottadito (see page 68 for the classic lamb version). They taste great with a bread and nut sauce inspired by the Turkish walnut condiment tarator. PS You are not allowed to make this recipe with farmed salmon. Not only will it support a dangerous industry that threatens our oceans with pollution, non-native fish escapes, and biological hazards, but it won't taste good, either.

Prepare a very hot charcoal grill. Give the grate a good scraping with a brush once hot. Soak a piece of paper towel with oil and, using tongs, rub it on the grate to thoroughly coat.

Coat both sides of the salmon steaks and the cut sides of the lemons with the olive oil. Season the salmon well with salt and freshly ground black pepper. Place the lemons on the grill cut side down. Place the salmon steaks on the hot grill and cook until they are very well seared, about 6½ to 7 minutes. Resist the urge to fiddle with them until they are well seared. Turn the steaks over and cook to desired doneness—about 2½ to 4 minutes on the second side; I like the steak centers to be darker pink than the exterior and would pull them on the early side; if you like an even opacity, cook on the longer end of the range. Remove the lemons from the grill when they are dramatically charred on the cut side.

To serve, swipe the hazelnut tarator across the bottom of a big serving platter (you will probably have more than you need for this recipe). Place the salmon atop the sauce and nestle the lemons among the steaks. Spoon the pickled cherry tomatoes on top, letting some of their juices run over the fish.

EL REY

keeping salmon wild

The world's oceans are in trouble—you probably know this already. It is hard to know how to eat sustainably in this moment, and all I know is that I do my best to lead by example both in my restaurants and at home. I'm always learning. We have long loved putting rich wild King (aka Chinook) salmon on our menus—it's so voluptuous and vivid, especially compared to the farmed salmon our customers from outside the Pacific Northwest are used to. I support aquaculture that is not harmful to the environment and native species, like shellfish farming or onshore closed-system fish farms. At this point, however, open-water pen farming like what is used for salmon is terrible. It pollutes the ocean with waste, antibiotics, and potential escape of non-native fish. Also, farmed salmon tastes bad. So I work only with wild-catch salmon.

But recently, we have been hearing more and more dire news about the near extinction of our region's Orca whales, whose primary source of nutrition is Chinook salmon, whose own numbers are looking really dire. Fewer and fewer Chinook make the swim back to rivers each year to spawn. So we took it off the menu in my restaurants. Instead we focused on lesser-known wild salmon including chum, pink, coho, and sockeye, and we are appreciating their own delicious nuances.

I try to support the food suppliers who are working to change the system, particularly here alongside the Salish Sea (that's the name given to the interconnected waterways of Washington and British Columbia, and named for the indigenous peoples of the region). Reef-net fishing, based on indigenous fishing methods and championed by my friend Riley Starks on Lummi Island, is an example of something promising in the seafood world. With reef nets, salmon are harvested close to the river mouths they are returning to, not way out at sea, which can only be accessed with diesel engines. At the reef, the net is pulled only when a salmon school has been spotted—no bycatch issues, and the fish are pulled out of the water at the waterline, with no long fight or penning, so they emerge cleaner than any other fish we receive—no bruises, no lacerations, just beautiful. There are several new reef-net fisheries developing as we write, and I am hoping that it can become a strong model for the future of salmon fishing. Check the Wild Fish Conservancy's website for updates on the state of the ocean and the most sustainable fishing methods. And Riley's beautiful reef-net salmon can be ordered from his website; see Resources, page 344.

pickles and other staples

buttered boiled potatoes

1½ pounds (680 g) whole small Yellow Finn
    potatoes
Salt
3 tablespoons unsalted butter
Freshly ground black pepper

Serves 4 to 6

Place the potatoes in a large pot of salted water
that covers the potatoes by at least 2 inches
(5 cm). Bring to a boil, then reduce the heat
to a simmer. Cook the potatoes until tender
at the center when pierced with a knife, about
10 minutes. Drain the potatoes and transfer to
a bowl. Melt the butter and toss the potatoes
with it, seasoning well with salt and pepper.

cilantro-jalapeño simple syrup

1 cup (200 g) sugar
1 bunch cilantro (stems and all)
2 jalapeños, halved lengthwise

Makes ¾ cup (180 ml)

In a small saucepan, combine 1 cup (240 ml)
water with the sugar, cilantro, and jalapeños
and bring to a boil. With a wooden spoon,
smash the jalapeños and the cilantro to
release their flavor.

Reduce the heat to a simmer and cook for
5 minutes. Strain. The syrup will keep in an
airtight container in the refrigerator for up
to a week.

crepes

2 large eggs
1½ cups (360 ml) whole milk
1 teaspoon sugar
½ teaspoon salt
¾ cup plus 1 tablespoon (100 g) buckwheat flour
¼ cup (30 g) all-purpose flour
¾ cup (1½ sticks/170 g) melted unsalted butter,
    cooled to lukewarm

Makes 3 cups (720 ml) batter, for about
*   12 (10-inch/25-cm) crepes*

In a blender, buzz the eggs with the milk,
sugar, and salt. Add the flours, blend well, and
finally, blend in ¼ cup (55 g) of the melted
butter. An immersion blender works wonder-
fully here, too, if you have one. Let the mixture sit overnight in the refrigerator.

Place a 10-inch (25-cm) crepe pan or black
steel pan over medium-high heat. Drizzle
with 1 to 2 teaspoons of the remaining ½ cup
(115 g) melted butter and swirl to cover the
pan. Have a plate ready nearby. Ladle about ¼
cup (60 ml) crepe batter into the pan. Tilt the
pan to move the batter around the whole pan,
making a circle. Cook on one side for 40 seconds, until set and slightly browned. Carefully
flip the crepe with an offset spatula or rubber
spatula. Cook 10 more seconds and move it to
the prepared plate. Repeat with the remaining
butter and batter.

fermented hot sauce

2 garlic cloves, peeled
1 pound (455 g) Fresno chiles, stemmed and
    seeded
1 red serrano pepper, stemmed and seeded
3 tablespoons sugar
3 tablespoons salt
1 cup (240 ml) olive oil
¾ cup (180 ml) cider vinegar

Makes about 2½ cups (600 ml)

In a food processor, pulse the garlic until roughly chopped, then add the chiles, sugar, and salt. Buzz to make an almost smooth puree. Pour into a clean 1-quart (1-L) glass jar, cover with cheesecloth, and secure it with a rubber band. Let the hot sauce sit at room temperature, lifting the cheesecloth and pressing down on the solids to make sure they are submerged in the brine daily. You will observe the bubbling activity of fermentation, and when the brine looks cloudy, in about 3 to 5 days, depending largely on temperature, the sauce is fermented and ready to finish.

After fermenting, blend the pepper puree with the olive oil and cider vinegar. Return the mixture to the glass jar and store in the refrigerator for several months.

grainy dijon vinaigrette

½ cup (120 g) grainy mustard
2 tablespoons finely minced shallot
⅓ cup (75 ml) Champagne vinegar
½ teaspoon salt, plus more to taste
Lots of freshly ground black pepper
1 cup (240 ml) really good olive oil

Makes about 2 cups (480 ml)

In a medium bowl, whisk together the mustard, shallot, vinegar, salt, and pepper. While whisking, slowly stream in the olive oil to emulsify. This can be stored in the refrigerator for 1 day.

guajillo chile salt

I love the tangy-spicy Mexican spice blend Tajín, which is happily available at most large grocery stores these days. It's a fantastic way to rim a glass to add a bit of heat and some tartness to a cocktail or a beer. This home-made salt is another favorite option, made with the fruity guajillo chile that possesses only a bit of spiciness.

¼ cup (60 g) kosher salt
2 tablespoons ground guajillo chile

Makes about ¼ cup (70 g)

In a small bowl, combine the salt and the chile powder. Transfer to an airtight jar until use; it will stay fresh and vibrant at room temperature for about a month.

hazelnut tarator

1 cup (135 g) hazelnuts, toasted, cooled
    (see page 20 for more on toasting nuts)
2 small garlic cloves, peeled
Zest of 1 whole lemon
1 tablespoon lemon juice
¾ cup (180 ml) olive oil
1 teaspoon salt, plus more to taste

Makes about 2 cups (480 ml)

In a blender, combine the hazelnuts, garlic, lemon zest, lemon juice, olive oil, ¼ cup (60 ml) water, and salt and pulse until chopped, pushing down the mixture occasionally to keep things moving. When it becomes a rough paste, puree continuously until smooth. Taste and adjust with more salt or lemon juice if desired. This sauce can be used right away, but it tastes even better after mellowing for an hour. Store any extra in the refrigerator for up to 2 days; it can be tossed with pasta and fresh herbs for a quick dinner.

hibiscus tea

¼ cup (9 g) hibiscus flowers (you can get
    hibiscus flowers from most health-focused
    groceries)

Makes 1½ cups (355 ml)

In a small pot, combine 2 cups (480 ml) water with the hibiscus flowers and bring to a boil. Reduce the heat to a simmer and cook for 20 minutes. Strain and chill. It can be kept in the refrigerator for 2 days.

homemade salt cod

2 pounds (910 g) fresh cod fillets
Kosher salt, about 4 cups (960 g)

Makes 2 pounds (910 g)

Remove the bones and trim off any flesh that is not bright white. Cut the fish into pieces 3 to 4 inches (7.5 to 10 cm) long. Cover the bottom of a baking dish large enough to hold all the cod with 1 or 2 cups (240 or 480 g) of salt. Lay the fish in a single layer, and then top with more salt to completely cover the fish. Cover with plastic wrap and store in the fridge for 4 hours, then remove and rinse the fish. The fish should be firm but not hardened from the salt bath. Place the fish on a double layer of paper towels to thoroughly dry.

horseradish cream

1 cup (240 ml) sour cream
½ teaspoon Dijon mustard
¼ cup (5 g) freshly grated horseradish root,
    grated on a Microplane
½ teaspoon lemon juice
Kosher salt and freshly ground black pepper

Makes 1 cup (240 g)

In a medium bowl, combine the sour cream, mustard, horseradish, lemon juice, and salt and pepper. The cream is best eaten the same day; it will discolor overnight.

lemon aioli

This makes a little more than you might eat with a pound of calamari: Use any extra on sandwiches or alongside some roast chicken.

2 large egg yolks
1 tablespoon freshly squeezed lemon juice
1 teaspoon salt
1 garlic clove, crushed
¾ cup (175 ml) extra-virgin olive oil
¾ cup (175 ml) canola oil
Salt and freshly ground black pepper

Makes about 2 cups (480 ml)

In a cylindrical quart container or large glass canning jar, place the egg yolks, lemon juice, salt, and garlic. Buzz together with an immersion blender until smooth. Add the olive oil and canola slowly and, starting at the bottom of the container, turn the immersion blender on and draw the blender gradually upward. Slowly move the blender up and down to emulsify all the ingredients. Taste and add salt and pepper to adjust the seasoning. If desired, thin the aioli with a tablespoon or two of cold water.

Cover with plastic wrap, putting the plastic right down on the surface of the aioli to keep it from forming a thick skin. Store in the refrigerator for up to 1 day before serving.

oyster aioli

3 oysters, shucked
2 large egg yolks
½ teaspoon Dijon mustard
2 teaspoons lemon juice
1 cup (240 ml) olive oil
Salt and freshly ground black pepper

Makes 2 cups (480 ml)

In a small skillet over medium heat, sauté the oysters until firm, about 5 minutes total. Let cool to room temperature.

In a cylindrical 1-quart (1-L) container or large glass canning jar, add the oysters, egg yolks, Dijon mustard, and lemon juice. Buzz with an immersion blender to chop the oysters thoroughly. Add the olive oil slowly and, starting at the bottom of the container, turn the immersion blender on and draw the blender gradually upward. Slowly move the hand blender up and down to emulsify all the ingredients. Taste and add salt and pepper. Store in the refrigerator for 1 day.

piccalilli

10 cups (1.3 kg) mixed vegetables (red peppers, cucumbers, zucchini, cauliflower, onion, celery), chopped into bite-size pieces
⅓ cup plus 1 tablespoon (110 g) kosher salt
3 cups (720 ml) apple cider vinegar
6 tablespoons (65 g) fine cornmeal
⅓ cup (50 g) ground turmeric
⅓ cup (50 g) mustard powder
1 tablespoon yellow mustard seeds
1 tablespoon coriander seeds, crushed
1 tablespoon cumin seeds, crushed
1 cup (200 g) sugar
3 tablespoons honey

Makes about 2½ quarts (2.5 L)

In a large bowl, combine the vegetables with ⅓ cup (90 g) of the salt. Cover with a tea towel and let sit in a cool place for 24 hours. The next day, rinse the vegetables with very cold water and drain well.

In a blender, combine ½ cup (120 ml) of the vinegar with the cornmeal, turmeric, mustard powder and seed, coriander seeds, and cumin seeds. Set aside.

In a 4- to 5-quart (4- to 5-L) nonreactive saucepan, combine the remaining vinegar with the sugar and honey and bring to a boil. Whisk in the spice paste and 1 tablespoon salt. Reduce the heat to medium and simmer for 2 to 3 minutes, stirring frequently.

Gently add the vegetables to the hot vinegar mixture. Remove from the heat and let cool before packing into airtight jars and storing in the refrigerator. The piccalilli will be better after sitting overnight and will keep for a week or two in a tightly sealed glass jar in the refrigerator.

pickled celery

4 celery stalks, sliced diagonally in ¼-inch
    (6-mm) slices
12 ounces (340 ml) white wine vinegar
2 bay leaves, fresh if possible
2 strips lemon zest, about 1 inch (2.5 cm) wide
2 tablespoons sugar

Makes 1 (1-quart/1-L) jar

Have the celery ready in a 1-quart (1-L) glass jar or other heatproof container.

In a small, nonreactive saucepan, combine 1 cup (240 g) water, the vinegar, bay leaves, lemon zest, and sugar and bring to a boil. Let boil for 2 minutes.

Pour the hot liquid over the celery. Let cool, then cover the container with its lid and refrigerate until use; the texture will be best if eaten within 2 weeks.

pickled fresno chiles

1 cup (240 ml) white wine vinegar
3 Fresno chiles, thinly sliced about ⅓ inch (3 mm)
    thick

Makes about 1¼ cups (300 ml)

In a small, nonreactive saucepan, bring the vinegar and ½ cup (120 ml) water to a boil. Stir in the chiles and cook until they turn translucent but remain a bit crunchy. Set aside to cool. The chiles in their liquid will keep stored in an airtight jar in the refrigerator for a week or two—I like adding them to scrambled egg tacos for breakfast.

pickled green tomatoes

3 pounds (1.4 kg) green tomatoes (or whatever
    you have left in your garden, really)
2 garlic cloves, halved
6 to 8 thyme sprigs
3 cups (720 ml) white wine vinegar
Bay leaf, fresh if available
2 tablespoons salt
2 tablespoons sugar
2 dried red chiles
½ teaspoon fennel seeds
1 teaspoon mustard seeds
1 teaspoon coriander seeds

Makes 3 or 4 (1-quart/1-L) jars

Have ready 3 or 4 sterilized 1-quart (1-L) glass canning jars and lids (depending on the size of your tomatoes, you may not need them all).

Cut the tomatoes in half, quarters, or slices, depending on the size (look for pieces about 1 inch/2.5 cm thick at the widest) and place them in the sterilized jars, filling to the "shoulders" of the jars. Add half a garlic clove to each jar and distribute the thyme sprigs among the jars. In a small saucepan, combine 1 cup (240 ml) water with the vinegar, bay leaf, salt, sugar, and all the spices. Bring to a boil, then reduce the heat and simmer for 5 minutes.

Gently fill each jar with the brine and cover with a lid. Let cool to room temperature and refrigerate for 3 to 5 days, when the tomatoes will be ready to eat. You can store the pickled tomatoes in the refrigerator for a couple of months, but their texture is best in the first month.

pickled onions

1 cup (240 ml) white wine vinegar
1 teaspoon sugar
2 sprigs thyme
10 small red torpedo onions, about 1 inch
    (2.5 cm) wide at the thickest point, peeled
    and whole, or 1 large red onion, peeled and
    cut into ¾-inch (2-cm) wedges

Makes 1 quart (1 L)

In a medium saucepan, bring the vinegar, ½ cup (120 ml) water, the sugar, and thyme to a boil. Add the onions, reduce the heat to a simmer, and cook for 3 to 4 minutes, until the onions are still crisp but a little translucent on the exterior. Remove from the heat and let cool completely. Store in an airtight container in the refrigerator for up to 1 month.

pickled sweet 100 cherry tomatoes

2 cups (480 ml) great-quality white wine vinegar
    (I like Katz)
3 tablespoons sugar
1 teaspoon salt
3 sprigs fresh summer savory or fresh thyme
1 garlic clove, cut in half
2 pints cherry tomatoes, if possible Sweet 100,
    stemmed

Makes about 2 (1-pint/480-ml) jars

In a pot, combine ¾ cup (180 ml) water with the vinegar, sugar, salt, savory, garlic, and tomatoes. Bring to a simmer and cook for about 10 minutes, enough for the garlic clove to soften.

Transfer the cherry tomatoes to nonreactive jars and pour the hot pickle brine over the tomatoes. Let sit for at least 2 days in the refrigerator, and then they are ready to serve.

pie pastry

2½ cups (315 g) all-purpose flour, sifted
1 teaspoon salt
1 cup (2 sticks/225 g) cold unsalted butter, cut
    into ½-inch (12-mm) chunks
½ cup (120 ml) ice water

*Makes enough for 1 double-crust 10-inch
    (25-cm) pie*

In a food processor, pulse the flour and salt to combine. Add half of the butter and pulse until pebbly. Add the remaining butter and pulse again; there should be a mix of butter fragments—some tiny, others more cornflake-size. Add ice water into the mixture a little at a time, stopping as soon as the dough comes together. Gather the mixture into a ball and divide evenly into two pieces. Wrap each half in plastic wrap, shaping into a disc as you do. Refrigerate for 1 hour before rolling; when well wrapped, the dough can be stored in the refrigerator for 2 or 3 days, or in the freezer for up to 1 month. Let frozen dough thaw in the refrigerator overnight before rolling.

poached eggs

Salt
½ teaspoon white wine vinegar
2 large eggs

Makes 2 eggs

In a medium saucepan, bring at least 4 inches (10 cm) water to a gentle boil with a pinch of salt and the vinegar. Adjust the heat to keep the water at an easy simmer. Carefully crack an egg into a small bowl and gently slide it into the water. Repeat with the other egg. Do not fidget with the eggs, but allow them to rise to the surface, no more than 3 minutes to get a perfectly runny yolk, keeping the water at a very low simmer. One at a time, remove the poached eggs from the water with a slotted spoon, touching the spoon to a clean kitchen towel to collect any extra water.

roasted serrano oil

5 serrano chiles
¾ cup neutral oil, such as canola or sunflower
6 sprigs Italian parsley

Makes about ¾ cup (180 ml)

In a heavy iron skillet over high heat, char the serranos, turning once or twice, until they blacken slightly on both sides and become slack. Let them cool for 5 minutes. Holding each pepper by the stem, use a knife to halve each pepper lengthwise and scrape the seeds and pith out. Cut off the stems.

Place the chiles in a blender with the oil and parsley. Buzz for 1 minute. Strain the oil mixture through a fine-mesh sieve, letting it drip for 10 minutes. Discard the solids. The oil can be prepared ahead and stored in an airtight container in the refrigerator for 3 days.

sage oil

½ cup (9 g) sage leaves
1½ cups (350 ml) grapeseed or sunflower seed oil

Makes 1½ cups (350 ml)

Have ready a medium bowl of ice water. Bring a medium saucepan of salted water to a boil. Submerge the sage leaves in the water and blanch just until they soften, about 15 seconds. Plunge into the ice bath and cool. When cool, squeeze the leaves well to dry, then chop coarsely.

In a blender, puree the blanched sage with the grapeseed oil until very smooth. Strain the oil through a fine-mesh sieve. The oil can be made up to 2 days ahead; store in an airtight container in the refrigerator. Let the oil come to room temperature before using.

salsa verde

2 garlic cloves, chopped
2 anchovy fillets
1 tablespoon chopped drained capers
½ teaspoon freshly ground black pepper
¾ teaspoon salt
1 teaspoon chile flakes
1 cup (20 g) packed chopped Italian parsley
    leaves
Finely grated zest of 1 lemon, about
    4 tablespoons
3 tablespoons lemon juice
1 cup (240 ml) olive oil

Makes 1½ cups (360 ml)

In a mortar and pestle, combine the garlic, anchovies, capers, black pepper, salt, and chile flakes. Mash together into a smooth paste. Stir in the parsley, lemon zest, lemon juice, and olive oil. Store in the refrigerator for up to 1 day.

seaweed butter

1 cup (2 sticks/225 g) good-quality unsalted
    butter (I like Kerrygold), at room
    temperature
Zest from 1 lemon
2 tablespoons green seaweed flakes (I use
    nori flakes, which are easy to find in Asian
    groceries and online)
½ teaspoon fine sea salt
¼ teaspoon ground cayenne pepper

Makes 1 cup (225 g)

In a stand mixer fitted with the paddle attachment (or with a bowl, a sturdy whisk, and a lot of arm power), whip the ingredients together until fluffy. Extra butter can be stored in the refrigerator for 1 week or frozen for 1 to 2 months. Let the butter come to room temperature before serving.

smooth smoked chile salsa roja

6 ounces (170 g total) dried chiles (including at least one chipotle, along with any others you like, such as guajillo, cascabel, or ancho), about 2 packed cups, no seeds or stems
2 whole garlic cloves, peeled
2 tablespoons piloncillo or brown sugar
¼ cup (60 ml) white wine vinegar
½ white onion, diced
Zest of 1 lime
1 teaspoon dried Mexican oregano
2½ teaspoons salt, plus more to taste
1 cup (240 ml) olive oil
Lime juice (optional)

Makes 2 cups (475 ml)

In a 3-quart (3-L) nonreactive saucepan, combine 3 cups (720 ml) water with the chiles, garlic, piloncillo, vinegar, onion, lime zest, and oregano. Bring to a boil, then reduce the heat to a lazy simmer. Cook for 1 hour.

Working in batches, if necessary, carefully transfer to a blender with the salt and buzz until very smooth—remove the small port on the top of the blender and blend on low to avoid splattering. While the machine is running, slowly drizzle in the olive oil to emulsify it. Check the seasoning—you may want to add a little lime juice and more salt. Store in an airtight container in the refrigerator for up to 1 month.

tomato sauce

2 (28-ounce/795-g) cans whole peeled tomatoes, or 5 cups (1.2 L) tomato passata
½ cup (120 ml) olive oil
4 garlic cloves, peeled
2 tablespoons fennel seeds, toasted and ground
1 teaspoon salt

Makes about 4 cups (1 L)

If using the whole tomatoes, use a blender to puree the tomatoes and juices until smooth. Measure out 5 cups (1.2 L) of the puree.

In a wide 3- to 4-quart (2.8- to 3.8-L) saucepan over medium, heat the olive oil. Drop in the garlic and toast until it starts to brown, about 4 minutes. Remove the garlic from the pan. Remove the pan from the heat and pour in the tomatoes, being careful to avoid their spatter. Add the fennel, then stir well. Cover and return the pot to the stove. Cook over low heat for 30 to 40 minutes, stirring occasionally, until the sauce is about applesauce-thick. Add more salt and reserve until ready for use. Store in the refrigerator in an airtight container for up to 1 week.

resources

ATLAS OLIVE OILS
Delicious, reasonably priced oils from
Morocco, especially if you buy a multiliter tin.
atlasoliveoils.us

BOB'S RED MILL
Classic Oregon resource for whole grains and
flours, including buckwheat and semolina.
bobsredmill.com

CAIRNSPRING MILLS
Our choice for freshly milled flours.
cairnspring.com

CHEFSHOP
For olive oils, capers, preserves, mustards,
olives, special oils, buckwheat flour, and
spices. chefshop.com

COCKTAIL KINGDOM
For cocktail shakers, glasses, strainers, and
ice tools. cocktailkingdom.com

DELAURENTI
Seattle's go-to specialty store for charcuterie,
cheese, tomato products, tinned fish,
and more also ships around the country.
delaurenti.com

HAMA HAMA COMPANY
Even if you live far from the Puget Sound,
you can have icy, glorious oysters shipped to
you by Hama Hama. hamahamaoysters.com

KING ARTHUR FLOUR
Always-reliable source of high-quality baking
ingredients: I love that they collaborate
with Washington's Bread Lab to continue
the research into the health and viability of
diverse grain crops. kingarthurflour.com

LUMMI ISLAND WILD
Out-of-this-world smoked salmon from
my friend Riley Stark's reef-net salmon
fishery off Lummi Island, Washington.
They also ship cooked Dungeness crab.
lummiislandwild.com

RANCHO GORDO
A dizzying variety of beans, both familiar
and rare varieties—also a great resource
for chilies and bean cooking advice.
ranchogordo.com

SEAFOOD WATCH
Guidance on what seafood to eat and what
to avoid—download their app for help while
traveling. seafoodwatch.org

VILLA JERADA
My friend Mehdi Boujrada imports wonderful
spices and olive oil from Morocco. He is now
bringing in a great tahini, too. villajerada.com

ZINGERMAN'S
Fanatically edited selection of beautiful
preserved vegetables, olive oils, cheeses,
charcuterie, and other specialties.
zingermans.com

ocean conservation organizations

POSTELSIA
postelsia.com

PUGET SOUNDKEEPER
pugetsoundkeeper.org

WILD FISH CONSERVANCY
wildfishconservancy.org

sea creatures restaurants

Bar Melusine

Barnacle

Bateau

Bistro Shirlee

Deep Dive

General Porpoise

Great State Burger

The Walrus and the Carpenter

Westward

The Whale Wins

Willmott's Ghost

eatseacreatures.com

acknowledgments

thank you! *grazie! merci! ¡gracias!*

There are so many people who have helped shape this book. I feel so lucky to have a collection of amazingly talented people near and far that fill my world with love, art, and delicious food and beverages.

I want to thank my family for their endless support, curiosity, and boundless hunger.

Mom and Dad, you really are the best parents.

Ryan, I love you, big brother!

Maggie and Mateo, watching you grow up and love food (especially oysters) makes me so very happy. Maggie, you are the best assistant!

Dan, for teaching me the art of a hamburger. Thank you for always believing in me.

To my book team! It makes me smile thinking about all the adventures, meals, airplanes, potato chips, donkeys, oysters, wine, and cocktails that we enjoyed together while making this book. Sara Dickerman, Jeremy Price, Jim Henkens and Jeffry Mitchell: I could not have done this without all of your incredible talents.

To all the new and old friends in my favorite places that made this book so special: Stephane and Martine Le Bozec, Thierry and Caroline Pic, Katie Parla, Jennifer McIlvaine, Diana Henry, Margo Henderson, Dorie and Michael Greenspan, and Dano and Karla Sanchez.

To the UW Rome Center in the Palazzo Pio: That time in Rome changed my life.

To the restaurants and bars that inspire me endlessly: Armando al Pantheon, Il Goccetto, L'Angolo Divino, Roscioli, Trattoria Da Cesare al Casaletto, Litro, Pizzarium Bonci, Forno Campo de' Fiori, Buvette, Au Passage, Le Grand Bain, Martin, Le Saint Sébastien, Café de la Nouvelle Mairie, Le Baratin, Robert et Denis Andronikou fish market, Spring, River Café, Rochelle Canteen, St. John, Bar Termini, Luca, Marksman Public House, Quality Chop House, Quality Wines, Zetter Townhouse, Barracuda Cantina, El Refugio, Jazamango. I can't wait to return.

To Bobby Palmquist and Carrie Omegna, lifelong Sea Creatures: Thanks for filling in all the gaps I missed while I was working on this project.

To Kitty Cowles for pushing me, always with a smile.

To Laura Dozier and the team at Abrams for fostering my vision.

To my Sea Creatures family, past and present: I have so much gratitude for all that you do.

To the guests that fill our restaurants with generous energy and allow us to cook and care for you.

To all the farmers, winemakers, fishermen and suppliers who make what we do so much easier.

To my business partners: Jeremy Price, Chad Dale and Ira Gerlich. What fun we have. Thank you for the continued support.

To the places that have taught me so much and inspired me for all these years: Rome, Paris, Normandy, London, Baja, and Seattle. You are so beautiful.

index

Editor: Laura Dozier
Designer: Jeremy Price
Production Manager: Anet Sirna-Bruder

Library of Congress Control Number: 2020943988
ISBN: 978-1-4197-4039-8
eISBN: 978-1-64700-259-6

Printed and bound in China

10 9 8 7 6 5 4 3 2 1

Abrams books are available at special discounts when purchased in quantity for premiums and promotions as well as fundraising or educational use. Special editions can also be created to specification. For details, contact specialsales@abramsbooks.com or the address below.

ABRAMS The Art of Books
195 Broadway, New York, NY 10007
abramsbooks.com

One last glance back after a
lingering meal at Luca, London